Bisma Parvez

The
NEW MUSLIM
WORKBOOK

The Interactive Guide to Building Your Relationship with Allah through Reflection and Prayer

ULYSSES PRESS

Published by:
Ulysses Press
PO Box 3440
Berkeley, CA 94703
www.ulyssespress.com

ISBN: 9-781-64604-415-3
Library of Congress Control Number: 2022936173

Printed in the United States
10 9 8 7 6 5 4 3 2 1

Acquisitions editor: Claire Sielaff
Managing editor: Claire Chun
Editor: Renee Rutledge
Proofreader: Janet Vail
Front cover design: Iqra Ashraf
Interior design and layout: Winnie Liu
Artwork: cover artwork © Iqra Ashraf; wings © MarShot/Shutterstock.com

بِسْمِ ٱللَّهِ ٱلرَّحْمَٰنِ ٱلرَّحِيمِ

In the name of Allah, the Most Gracious, the Most Merciful

*I dedicate this book first and foremost in the name of my Lord, Allah
(swt), who has allowed me by His utmost mercy to share these words
that may be beneficial to anyone who reads them. Any good you receive
is from your Lord and any errors are from His humble servant.*

To Enaya, whose free spirit and kind heart never ceases to amaze me.

To Ibrahim, whose love and protection has never let me down.

To Tuba, my person.

*And to Syed and Saeeda Parvez, who sacrificed their life
for their children: I couldn't ask for better parents.*

*May our Lord shower His immense blessings and
mercy upon you in this life and the next.*

Ameen.

CONTENTS

INTRODUCTION

Assalamu alaikum!

Whether you're absolutely new to Islam or have been learning about it for a while, whether you're a new Muslim or old, you've likely heard the Islamic greeting meaning "peace and blessings upon you." So I start this book with Bismillah, which means "in the name of Allah (swt)," and wishing you peace and blessings.

There are a few reasons you might be here:

1. You're either a member of my family or a friend

2. You're interested in Islam

3. You're a new Muslim

4. You're a born Muslim finding your way again

If you're one of the latter three, that's a great start. Maybe you are in search of something: answers, peace, faith. For whatever reason, you found this book, or maybe it found its way to you. And every step you took to get to this book, to this page is a huge step in the right direction. It was no accident. God wanted you to get to this moment.

Let me introduce myself: My name is Bisma, and I am a Muslim—not necessarily a super-smart, absolutely amazing one either (though I do tend to think I'm a kind person with a great heart who loves her Lord). I have two awesome kids who drive me crazy from time to time but are amazing and beautiful. I have loving parents who still try to tell me what to do even though I'm a full-grown adult now, but I wouldn't have it any other way. I wear many hats: I am a mother, a daughter, a sister, a friend, a radiation therapist, a journalist, a writer, a content creator, but most importantly, I'm your average, run-of-the-mill Muslim born into this beautiful religion that I keep near and dear to my heart.

By now, it's likely you know that Muslims are just regular folks living their lives, going to work, raising their kids to be decent human beings, Netflix and chilling, and most importantly, believing in one God and His final messenger.

I must warn you, though, in case I haven't already made it clear, in no way, shape, or form am I an expert on all things Islam. I'm not a scholar or an Islamic teacher, and I haven't studied Islam professionally. I'm literally just a struggling, everyday Muslim trying my best—and sometimes that's *exactly* who you need to hear from when you're starting something new or finding your way. Sometimes, you need to hear from someone who's walked the same path, felt the same confusion, and has the same purpose.

But that also means that some things I say may not be *exactly* how every other Muslim sees them. Muslims aren't a part of a cult—we don't believe in or practice everything the exact same way. When it comes to the details, we tend to practice our faith in the best way we can that makes sense to us, but the foundations of Islam are the same, and that's what we'll focus on: things like what we believe and why we believe in this beautiful journey called Islam. Throughout the workbook, I will share Quranic verses and their translations, mostly by Dr. Mustafa Khattab from The Clear Quran.

If you get any benefit from this book, that is due to Allah (swt) alone. And if there are any mistakes, those are from my own shortcomings, and I apologize in advance.

Remember, this book is to help you understand how to navigate being a Muslim, and while our destination may be the same, the paths we take and the obstacles we face may differ. Now, brace yourselves and throw your misconceptions out the door, the window, or whatever happens to be near you. Get prepared for the enlightenment God has written for you, from my fingertips to your minds. And let's continue with the name of Allah (swt): Bismillah!

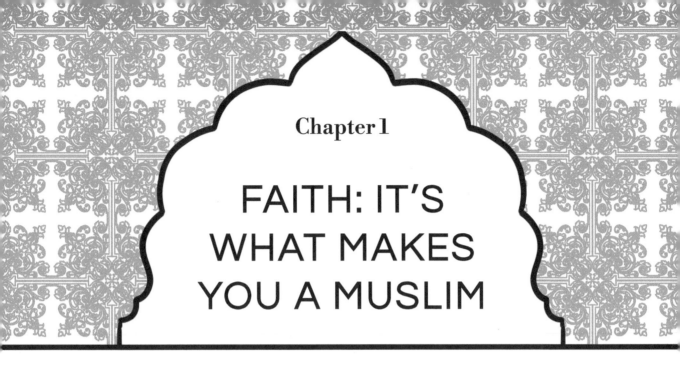

Chapter 1

FAITH: IT'S WHAT MAKES YOU A MUSLIM

What brings you here?

This might be a rhetorical question because I truly believe what brings anyone to Islam, other than God's guidance, of course, is faith. There's something in your heart—a feeling, a belief, a glimmer of hope—telling you that Islam is the answer, and belief in Allah (swt) is the thing that was or is missing from your life.

Allah (swt) is the name, the title, the way we refer to God. While I use "God" and "Allah (swt)" interchangeably in this book, in Arabic, "Allah (swt)" means the one and only God. SWT is short for *subhanahu wa ta'ala*, an Arabic term which means "the most glorified, the most high." We use this term as a way to continuously honor Him, and you will see it throughout the book. Not only does the term honor God, we also get good deeds every time we say (or read) it!

Whether you're newly interested in Islam or already a Muslim, the first thing to understand is what Islam really is because it's more than a religion: it is a way of life. It's not just a handbook of dos and don'ts, cans and cannots, but rather it's the way we choose to live because we believe in a higher power—Allah (swt). The beauty of Islam is that it's not exclusively connected with any race, country, or person. Anyone—regardless of age, nationality, ethnicity, gender, or language—can be a Muslim. You can be born into the religion or find it later in life. The beauty of Islam is that no one can judge your faith but Allah (swt), your Most Merciful Master. No one can judge what is in your heart, though many may try.

All religions have rules and regulations, but that's not what makes someone believe in it, follow it, and love it. If anything, that's the kind of stuff that makes you wonder why you are doing something in the first place. But any religion is all about faith in something or someone bigger than yourself.

God created everything: the sun, the skies, the heaven and the earth, and everything and everyone in between. And from all His creations, humans—you and me—are the greatest. When the human being was created, God instilled a want, a desire, a belief in our souls to submit to Him. But after that light was placed, we were the only creation who were offered a choice; we are the only ones who have free will. So we can either submit to God or go our own way. And when a human being chooses to submit themselves to God, even though they have a choice not to believe in God at all, that is the act of accepting Islam. Islam is giving yourself in submission to God.

What's important, though, is what *you* think and feel in this moment. The best way to start your journey in order to align your body with your soul's inclination is to reflect. What events, whether recent or way in the past, have happened in your life that have led you to have faith in a higher being, particularly Allah (swt)? Think about what brought you here: to this day, this moment, this book, this page.

Exercise: Digging Deep

Why am I here? What series of events brought my mind, soul, and body to Islam? Am I sure I'm in the right place?

_____

_____

_____

_____

_____

_____

_____

_____

_____

_____

_____

_____

_____

_____

_____

_____

_____

The Original Testimony

Now that you've thought about what brought your mind, soul, and body to this place, there's one thing to remember: you are not here by chance. While the series of events that you just reflected on did indeed bring you to the realization that you need Allah (swt), there is one event that you don't remember—the very first event that brought your soul to God: the original testimony.

This feeling to fulfill yourself, this calling to turn to your Lord, this light that wants to shine brighter isn't there by pure luck. It was placed in your heart by Allah (swt) even before you were placed on this Earth. Before your physical body took its first breath, your soul testified that Allah (swt) is your Lord.

In the Quran, Allah's (swt) holy book, Allah (swt) says:

وَإِذْ أَخَذَ رَبُّكَ مِن بَنِىٓ ءَادَمَ مِن ظُهُورِهِمْ ذُرِّيَّتَهُمْ وَأَشْهَدَهُمْ عَلَىٰٓ أَنفُسِهِمْ أَلَسْتُ بِرَبِّكُمْ قَالُوا بَلَىٰ ۩١٧٢ شَهِدْنَآ أَن تَقُولُوا يَوْمَ ٱلْقِيَـٰمَةِ إِنَّا كُنَّا عَنْ هَـٰذَا غَـٰفِلِينَ ○

And remember when your Lord brought forth from the loins of the children of Adam their descendants and had them testify regarding themselves. Allah asked, "Am I not your Lord?" They replied, "Yes, You are! We testify." He cautioned, "Now you have no right to say on Judgment Day, "We were not aware of this." (Quran 7:172)

This is how we know every one of us is born with a natural belief in Allah (swt) and a natural inclination to worship Him alone. This inclination is called *fitrah*.

Our fitrah is our biggest blessing because it is what brings us consistently back toward seeking Allah's (swt) pleasure. It's our head start, our bonus, our cheat sheet. If we were left on our own to figure it out and find Allah (swt) without our fitrah, it would be near impossible. What a blessing that Allah (swt) did not send us into the world without a map, a light, a guide!

Then, it's our faith and actions along the way that either bring us closer to our Lord or take us away from Him. Our soul naturally wants to submit to Allah (swt) because our souls have already been shown this truth, realized it, testified to it, and want to commit to it. But it is our egos and our bodies that seek immediate worldly pleasures, causing an unrest and unease within ourselves.

A Series of Fortunate Events

It may feel like you've had to face horrible things to get to this point: maybe abuse, loss, emptiness, betrayal, or loneliness. Maybe you had a hard life, felt the death of a loved one, or maybe things just weren't making sense or aligning with what you were taught to believe. Maybe you had everything but still wanted to feel *something*. Whatever it was, whether your reflections and memories felt "good" or "bad," I like to believe that they were in fact a series of fortunate events.

Why?

Because they brought you near God, and there is nothing more beautiful in this life, and nothing more comforting, than relying on the one who created it.

If we were able to feel fulfilled without God, we would never search for God. How sad it would be to never feel nearness to the one who created everything. That's why even those who seemingly have it all—money, fame, power, success, love—still feel an emptiness. Why do famous actors who seem to have the perfect life or successful artists who have fans all over the world drown in drugs or alcohol, or even commit suicide? How is it possible that someone who has all the pleasures of the world, still takes their own life? Because worldly pleasures do not equate to inner peace. True fulfillment comes when you have Allah (swt) in your heart, and that is why any event that brings you closer to God is a blessing.

In this world, "good" and "bad" are relative. What is good for one person may be bad for another, and what we think is good for us could turn out to be the worst thing that could happen to us because we don't know what it will lead to. As Muslims, we know the ultimate goodness is closeness to God because our time on this Earth is short. This world is not our ultimate goal. So whatever brings us to success in the akhirah (the afterlife) is good, even if it means some difficulty in this life.

In the Quran, Allah (swt) tells us the story of Prophet Musa (alay-hi 's-salām), or Moses (peace be upon him), and Al-Khidr, a servant of Allah (swt) who was given special knowledge of the unseen, such as certain things that would happen in the future.

فَوَجَدَا عَبْدًا مِّنْ عِبَادِنَا آتَيْنَٰهُ رَحْمَةً مِّنْ عِندِنَا وَعَلَّمْنَٰهُ مِن لَّدُنَّا عِلْمًا ٦٥

There they found a servant of Ours, to whom We had granted mercy from Us and enlightened with knowledge. (Quran 18:65)

Musa (as) accompanied Al-Khidr on a journey to learn from him. However, Musa (as) was told that he wouldn't have the patience to learn because he would see things he wouldn't understand. Musa (as) promised to be patient and not question Al-Khidr and was therefore allowed to join Al-Khidr.

Here are the three events that took place:

1. Al-Khidr and Musa (as) boarded a ship, and Al-Khidr made a hole in the ship. Musa (as) protested, "Have you done this to drown its people? You have certainly done a terrible thing!" (Quran 18:71)

2. Next on the journey, they saw a boy and Al-Khidr took his life. Musa (as) protested, "Have you killed an innocent soul, who killed no one? You have certainly done a horrible thing." (Quran 18:74)

3. Lastly they came into a town and asked the townspeople for food, but the townspeople didn't help them. In that same town there was a wall falling apart, and Al-Khidr fixed it. Musa (as) protested, "If you wanted, you could have demanded a fee for this." (Quran 18:77)

After the third strike, Musa (as) was not allowed to continue on the journey with Al-Khidr but Al-Khidr did explain his actions before parting ways.

1. A hole in the ship: The ship belonged to poor people. However, there was a tyrannical king who was seizing every ship he found that was in good shape, and Al-Khidr damaged their ship to save it from being taken away.

2. Killing the boy: The boy's parents were true believers, but the boy was not and would've pressured them into disbelieving. Instead, the parents would be blessed with another child, more caring and a believer. Murder is not allowed in Islam by any human, but remember Al-Khidr was not human. He was given divine knowledge to protect the future of a family and as a lesson to a prophet. So this was a rare and extreme circumstance.

3. Fixing the wall: The wall belonged to two orphans, whose father was very righteous. There was a treasure under the wall that belonged to the orphans. Had it crumbled, their treasure would've been looted. This way their treasure was protected until they got older and could take what belonged to them.

It's important to understand that Al-Khidr did not make these decisions on his own from his own free will. This was knowledge and guidance given to him from Allah (swt) because only our Lord truly knows the benefit and "good" in a seemingly "bad" situation. Al-Khidr was simply following the divine knowledge given to him by Allah (swt).

Exercise: A Lesson Learned

What are some lessons and takeaways that you learned from the story of Musa (as) and Al-Khidr?

TOPIC	LESSON
Impatience	
"Good" vs. "bad"	
Limited knowledge	

TOPIC	LESSON
Trusting God	
Keeping your promises	

As humans, our knowledge is limited, so it's hard to see the "goodness" in a tough situation. Allah (swt), on the other hand, is the All Knower: He knows the past, the present, and the future. He knows what we know not. This is why we trust that whatever happens to us, seemingly "good" or "bad," as long as we are trying to please Allah (swt), is beneficial for us, even if we don't understand it. Our Lord's plan is the best plan; it's why we are told to have patience in a "bad" situation, because we have no idea what we are being saved from and what good will come because of it.

While the story of Al-Khidr shows us how much we don't understand, especially in the moment, there are times we are given the reasons or see good afterward. And even though we do not have our own personal Al-Khidr to explain the reasonings for what we have faced, sometimes we can look back once our hardship is over and see the goodness ourselves. Many times, things end up making sense. So those seemingly bad things that have happened to you—the hardships, the tests, the tears, the losses—that brought you to this moment to seek God: were they actually "bad?"

Or were they a blessing in disguise?

Exercise: Blessings in Disguise

Look back at the times you felt your lowest or were going through a hardship. In retrospect, you should be able to see some goodness that came out of those times, be it patience, a better option, closeness to God, a new friend, a different job, or success where you didn't imagine. Write down what your test was and how it ended up being a blessing.

THE TEST	THE BLESSING

These "aha" moments in life help us look back and understand that what happened made complete sense. It can give you so much comfort and ease knowing that a hardship or disappointment brought you to something even better, and we praise God in those moments:

"Thank God I didn't marry so-and-so! Did you see how he treats his wife?"

"Thank God I didn't end up getting that job. The company went under after four months, and I have a much more stable and secure position in this company instead!"

"Thank God I didn't get into the car. The driver ended up getting into a car accident. I truly feel like God saved me!"

"Thank God I didn't go downtown Friday night with my coworkers. I ended up going to the mosque instead and made an amazing new friend. I wouldn't have met her otherwise."

But remember, while it's such a blessing and gift to understand the benefit of a situation, you don't always get it. You don't always get that clarity. Sometimes, it still won't make sense 10, 20, even 30 years later. Sometimes you'll still pine for a different outcome. But the great thing about the moments that *do* make sense is that they bring solace in the times that we don't understand because they serve as a reminder that Allah (swt) always does what's best for us.

This is how we as humans learn to trust Allah (swt), lean on Him, and turn to Him because if everything made sense, we wouldn't need to have blind trust. And if nothing made sense, then we'd have no hope and nothing to reassure us. Allah (swt) created a perfect balance of the "aha" moments and the moments that require us to trust unknowingly. This balance is not the same for everyone: it is based on our individual capacity to understand. This is why we aren't all given the same problems, the same gifts, the same hopes, or the same outcomes.

In the Quran (2:286), Allah (swt) says,

اَهَعِسُو آلِا اَسِهَنَ ۚ ةَللَا اُفِـلِلَكُي آل

Allah does not burden a soul beyond that it can bear.

Allah (swt) knows us better than we know ourselves. After all, He created us! This is why we trust Allah's (swt) plan—because we truly believe in our heart of hearts that there is no better plan.

This is *tawakkul*.

Chapter Summary Exercise: Never Stop Learning

What is something new I learned from this chapter, either about Islam or myself?

_____

_____

_____

_____

_____

What am I grateful for today?

_____

_____

_____

_____

_____

How did I lean on Allah (swt) today?

_____

_____

_____

_____

_____

Is there anyone I can forgive today? Or is there someone I should reach out to for forgiveness?

_____

_____

_____

_____

_____

THE NEW MUSLIM WORKBOOK

Chapter 2

TAWAKKUL: IT'S WHEN YOU TRUST GOD

What is trust?

Trust is a firm and unwavering belief in something or someone. You cannot have tawakkul without complete trust in Allah (swt). Tawakkul is a firm belief that Allah's (swt) plan is the best plan. It's a firm belief that Allah (swt) has your back and no matter what happens, as long as your faith in Allah (swt) does not waver, you'll be okay.

There are some relationships where trust has to be earned and proven. This could be one with a neighbor or a friend, for example. That relationship starts with a clean slate on which trust can be built over time. However, some relationships come with built-in trust. The implication with such relationships, often blood relationships like with parents or siblings, is that you *should* trust each other—the blood relationship implies an inherent trust.

But whether the trust is inherent or built, it can always be broken, which is what makes all of our relationships fragile. Trust is not a constant and not a guarantee in any relationship except our relationship with Allah (swt): our trust in him is our tawakkul.

Exercise: Trust Circle

Think about those in your life you trust most. It can be family or friends. It can be someone who was given inherent trust and didn't break it, or it can be someone who earned your trust over time. In the circle below, write your name in the middle and the names of those you trust and their qualities in the spaces provided.

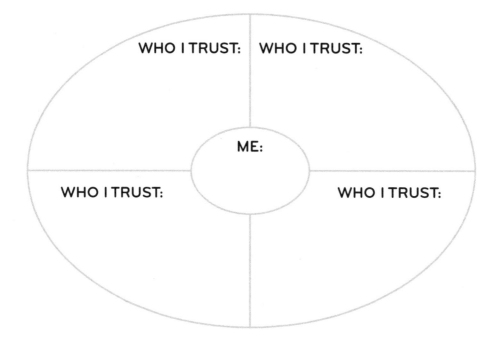

Looking over your trust circle, are there any qualities that overlap among those you trust? This is a great way to visualize the closest people to you, who you might turn to in a time of need, and why you trust them to be helpful. Maybe they have shown their loyalty to you. Maybe they were there to help you get through a challenging time. Maybe they are compassionate or smart. Whatever it is, the people we trust have to be able to provide some sort of support—physical, spiritual, emotional, or mental—for us to turn to them in our time of need. And depending on the problem, we may turn to a different person because each person has their own strengths.

But the reason tawakkul is the ultimate inherent trust is because Allah (swt) can and does provide support in every aspect of our life, no matter the kind of problem we are having and no matter what our need is. Allah (swt) has all the answers, so why wouldn't we trust Him the most?

Not only should we trust Allah (swt) truly and completely, we need to understand that there would never be a reason not to trust Him. Even when things don't make sense and it feels like we've been abandoned, our trust still never wavers. Your tawakkul should be so strong that you would mistrust yourself before you would mistrust Allah (swt).

So how can you have tawakkul?

The first thing to understand is that you don't just *have* tawakkul, you practice it. Having trust cannot simply be lip service. Just because you say you have tawakkul doesn't actually mean you believe it, day in, day out, especially when things get tough. It is easy to believe that we trust Allah (swt) when things are going well, but it's when we are in the eye of the storm that our tawakkul is truly tested.

Exercise: Who Helps You Through?

Can you think of a time when you were in desperate need? Was there ever a time when you felt the world was dark and you were overwhelmed? How did you make it out of that problem? Did you pray to a higher power for help? What actions did you take and how did things work out? Looking back, do you believe that Allah (swt) is the one that gave you the strength, the wit, the perseverance to make it through?

_____

_____

_____

_____

_____

_____

When we look back at our lives and how we made it through our hardships—because we did, otherwise we wouldn't be here right now—it should be clear that Allah (swt) helped us get out of our toughest situations. Allah (swt) provided physical assistance. Allah (swt) provided spiritual strength. Allah (swt) provided us with the mental capabilities. Remembering our past hardships and how we made it out of them should help us have trust in Allah (swt) when we're going through our current tests and trials. Because the truth is, being a Muslim, whether you are new or just renewing your faith, is in fact a test. It will not always be easy, but it will always be fruitful. Tawakkul will be your baseline and lifeline in the journey of living the life of the middle path: Islam.

99 Names

To trust Allah (swt) you must first get to know Him. Allah (swt) has many names and attributes that He has shared with us in the Holy Quran so that we may get to know Him and understand who our Lord is. Allah (swt) is often said to have 99 names, but some scholars believe He is not limited to 99. Either way, we do know 99 of them so if we do not attempt to get to know the characteristics and attributes of our Creator, then how can we learn to trust Him? It isn't because He is lacking but because we lack knowledge about our Lord that it makes us too weak to learn tawakkul.

Once we know Allah's (swt) names and attributes, we can call Him by his beautiful names especially as they pertain to what we need.

If we need to trust Allah's (swt) plan while we are in poverty, we can call him by *Ar-Razzaaq*, The Provider.

If we need to trust Allah's (swt) plan when we have been wronged by someone, we can call him by *Al-Hakam* and *Al-Fattaah*, The Giver of Justice and The Judge.

If we need to trust Allah's (swt) plan while we are feeling lost or don't know what decision to make, we can call him by *Al-Haadi*, The Guide.

Knowing Allah's (swt) attributes is the first step to understanding His power so we can truly understand that we are in the best and most capable hands.

These are the 99 names of Allah (swt):

NAME/ ATTRIBUTE	TRANSLITERATION	MEANING
1. الرَّحْمَٰنُ	AR-RAHMAAN	The Most Merciful
2. الرَّحِيمُ	AR-RAHEEM	The Bestower of Mercy
3. الْمَلِكُ	AL-MALIK	The King and Owner of Dominion
4. الْقُدُّوسُ	AL-QUDDUS	The Absolutely Pure
5. السَّلَامُ	AS-SALAM	The Perfection and The Giver of Peace
6. الْمُؤْمِنُ	AL-MU'MIN	The One Who Gives Faith and Security
7. الْمُهَيْمِنُ	AL-MUHAYMIN	The Guardian, The Witness, The Overseer
8. الْعَزِيزُ	AL-AZEEZ	The All-Mighty
9. الْجَبَّارُ	AL-JABBAR	The Compeller, The Restorer
10. الْمُتَكَبِّرُ	AL-MUTAKABBIR	The Supreme, The Majestic
11. الْخَالِقُ	AL-KHAALIQ	The Creator, The Maker
12. الْبَارِئُ	AL-BAARI'	The Originator
13. الْمُصَوِّرُ	AL-MUSAWWIR	The Fashioner
14. الْغَفَّارُ	AL-GHAFFAR	The All- and Oft-Forgiving
15. الْقَهَّارُ	AL-QAHHAR	The Subduer, The Ever-Dominating
16. الْوَهَّابُ	AL-WAHHAAB	The Giver of Gifts
17. الرَّزَّاقُ	AR-RAZZAAQ	The Provider
18. الْفَتَّاحُ	AL-FATTAAH	The Opener, The Judge

NAME/ ATTRIBUTE	TRANSLITERATION	MEANING
19. اَلْعَلِيمُ	AL-ALEEM	The All-Knowing, The Omniscient
20. اَلْقَابِضُ	AL-QAABID	The Withholder
21. اَلْبَاسِطُ	AL-BAASIT	The Extender
22. اَلْخَافِضُ	AL-KHAAFIDH	The Reducer, The Abaser
23. اَلرَّافِعُ	AR-RAAFI'	The Exalter, The Elevator
24. اَلْمُعِزُّ	AL-MU'IZZ	The Honorer, The Bestower
25. اَلْمُذِلُّ	AL-MUZIL	The Dishonorer, The Humiliator
26. اَلسَّمِيعُ	AS-SAMEE'	The All-Hearing
27. اَلْبَصِيرُ	AL-BASEER	The All-Seeing
28. اَلْحَكَمُ	AL-HAKAM	The Judge, The Giver of Justice
29. اَلْعَدْلُ	AL-'ADL	The Utterly Just
30. اَللَّطِيفُ	AL-LATEEF	The Subtle One, The Most Gentle
31. اَلْخَبِيرُ	AL-KHABEER	The Acquainted, The All-Aware
32. اَلْحَلِيمُ	AL-HALEEM	The Most Forbearing
33. اَلْعَظِيمُ	AL-'ATHEEM	The Magnificent, The Supreme
34. اَلْغَفُورُ	AL-GHAFOOR	The Forgiving, The Exceedingly Forgiving
35. اَلشَّكُورُ	ASH-SHAKOOR	The Most Appreciative
36. اَلْعَلِيُّ	AL-'ALEE	The Most High, The Exalted
37. اَلْكَبِيرُ	AL-KABEER	The Greatest, The Most Grand

NAME/ ATTRIBUTE	TRANSLITERATION	MEANING
38. أَلْحَفِيظُ	AL-HAFEEDH	The Preserver, The All-Heedful and All-Protecting
39. أَلْمُقِيتُ	AL-MUQEET	The Sustainer
40. أَلْحَسِيبُ	AL-HASEEB	The Reckoner, The Sufficient
41. أَلْجَلِيلُ	AL-JALEEL	The Majestic
42. أَلْكَرِيمُ	AL-KAREEM	The Most Generous, The Most Esteemed
43. أَلرَّقِيبُ	AR-RAQEEB	The Watchful
44. أَلْمُجِيبُ	AL-MUJEEB	The Responsive One
45. أَلْواسِعُ	AL-WAASI'	The All-Encompassing, The Boundless
46. أَلْحَكِيمُ	AL-HAKEEM	The All-Wise
47. أَلْوَدُودُ	AL-WADOOD	The Most Loving
48. أَلْمَجِيدُ	AL-MAJEED	The Glorious, The Most Honorable
49. أَلْباعِثُ	AL-BA'ITH	The Resurrector, The Raiser of the Dead
50. أَلشَّهِيدُ	ASH-SHAHEED	The All and The Ever-Witnessing
51. أَلْحَقُّ	AL-HAQQ	The Absolute Truth
52. أَلْوَكِيلُ	AL-WAKEEL	The Trustee, The Disposer of Affairs
53. أَلْقَوِيُّ	AL-QAWIYY	The All-Strong
54. أَلْمَتِينُ	AL-MATEEN	The Firm, The Steadfast
55. أَلْوَلِيُّ	AL-WALIYY	The Protecting Associate

NAME/ ATTRIBUTE	TRANSLITERATION	MEANING
56. اَلْحَمَيدُ	AL-HAMEED	The Praiseworthy
57. اَلْمُحْصِيُ	AL-MUHSEE	The All-Enumerating, The Counter
58. اَلْمُبْدِئُ	AL-MUBDI	The Originator, The Initiator
59. اَلْمُعِيدُ	AL-MU'ID	The Restorer, The Reinstater
60. اَلْمُحْيِىْ	AL-MUHYEE	The Giver of Life
61. اَلْمُمِيتُ	AL-MUMEET	The Bringer of Death, The Destroyer
62. اَلْحَىُّ	AL-HAYY	The Ever-Living
63. اَلْقَيُّومُ	AL-QAYYOOM	The Sustainer, The Self-Subsisting
64. اَلْواجِدُ	AL-WAAJID	The Perceiver
65. اَلْماجِدُ	AL-MAAJID	The Illustrious, The Magnificent
66. اَلْواحِدُ	AL-WAAHID	The One
67. اَلْأَحَدَ	AL-AHAD	The Unique, The Only One
68. اَلصَّمَدُ	AS-SAMAD	The Eternal, The Satisfier of Needs
69. اَلْقَادِرُ	AL-QADIR	The Capable, The Powerful
70. اَلْمُقْتَدِرُ	AL-MUQTADIR	The Omnipotent
71. اَلْمُقَدِّمُ	AL-MUQADDIM	The Expediter, The Promoter
72. اَلْمُؤْخَرُ	AL-MU'AKHKHIR	The Delayer, The Retarder
73. اَلْأَوَّلُ	AL-AWWAL	The First
74. اَلْآخِرُ	AL-AAKHIR	The Last
75. اَلظّاهِرُ	AZ-DHAAHIR	The Manifest

NAME/ ATTRIBUTE	TRANSLITERATION	MEANING
76. اَلْبَاطِنُ	AL-BAATIN	The Hidden One, Knower of the Hidden
77. اَلْوَالِي	AL-WAALI	The Governor, The Patron
78. اَلْمُتَعَالِي	AL-MUTA'ALI	The Self-Exalted
79. اَلْبَرُّ	AL-BARR	The Source of Goodness, The Kind Benefactor
80. اَلتَّوَّابُ	AT-TAWWAB	The Ever-Pardoning, The Relenting
81. اَلْمُنْتَقِمُ	AL-MUNTAQIM	The Avenger
82. اَلْعَفُوُّ	AL-'AFUWW	The Pardoner
83. اَلرَّؤُوفُ	AR-RA'OOF	The Most Kind
84. مَالِكُ الْمُلْكُ	MAALIK-UL-MULK	The Master of the Kingdom, The Owner of the Dominion
85. ذُو الْجَلَالِ وَالْإِكْرَامُ	DHUL-JALAALI WAL-IKRAAM	The Possessor of Glory and Honor, The Lord of Majesty and Generosity
86. اَلْمُقْسِطُ	AL-MUQSIT	The Equitable, The Requiter
87. اَلْجَامِعُ	AL-JAAMI'	The Gatherer, The Uniter
88. اَلْغَنِيُّ	AL-GHANIYY	The Self-Sufficient, The Wealthy
89. اَلْمُغْنِيُ	AL-MUGHNI	The Enricher
90. اَلْمَانِعُ	AL-MANI'	The Withholder
91. اَلضَّارُ	AD-DHARR	The Distresser, The Corrector
92. اَلنَّافِعُ	AN-NAFI'	The Propitious, The Benefactor
93. اَلنُّورُ	AN-NUR	The Light, The Illuminator
94. اَلْهَادِي	AL-HAADI	The Guide

NAME/ ATTRIBUTE	TRANSLITERATION	MEANING
95. ٱلْبَدَيعُ	AL-BADEE'	The Incomparable Originator
96. ٱلْبَاقِي	AL-BAAQI	The Ever-Surviving, The Everlasting
97. ٱلْوَارِثُ	AL-WAARITH	The Inheritor, The Heir
98. ٱلرَّشِيدُ	AR-RASHEED	The Guide, The Infallible Teacher
99. ٱلصَّبُورُ	AS-SABOOR	The Forbearing, The Patient

I believe trust in Allah (swt) requires four foundational beliefs: acceptance of your limitations, acknowledgment of Allah's (swt) divine knowledge, personal efforts, and unwavering belief in Allah's (swt) plan.

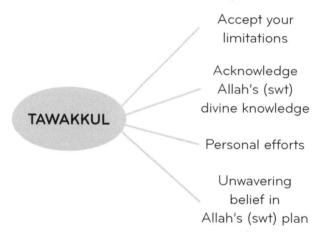

Accept Your Limitations

Tawakkul goes back to understanding that we have limited knowledge, just like Musa (as), who questioned Al-Khidr's actions. No matter how smart we are or how many degrees we hold, even if one is a prophet like Musa (as) himself, we will never have knowledge of everything in this world and we most certainly can never know the future.

When we are in a hardship or any difficult situation, filled with worry and fear, we truly understand our limitations: we cannot make anything happen. No matter how hard we try, we cannot guarantee the outcome. Things that we were normally able to do on any given day can become difficult or impossible when we fall ill or get hurt. Things we are able to remember every day, we sometimes completely forget: a name of a person or where we put a certain object. These are signs from God that we are not capable of doing anything on our own, not even thinking, unless He wills it and allows it to happen.

There are times when everything is going wrong and we have no idea what to do anymore because we've tried everything and have even asked people for help. It is usually in these moments that we look up to the sky with complete humility and call out to God for help. It is in the acceptance of our limitations and shortcomings that we realize we need hope from a higher power.

Think of your breath. The one you took just now. The one you took when you woke up this morning and the breath you will take before you fall asleep. Think of the breaths you take while you are sleeping. On average, we take about 22,000 breaths a day.

22,000!

We should be excellent breathers. And we are. We do it without thinking.

But haven't there been times when you've gotten so sick you could barely take your next breath, when breathing felt like the most difficult thing in the world? In those moments, we realize that it isn't up to us if we can take our next breath. Something we do without thinking 22,000 times a day, we cannot make happen anymore.

We realize that it was never us that allowed the next breath. It was our Sustainer. It is a truly humbling experience to accept that we can't even take our next breath if Allah (swt) does not will it.

But that realization can also cause despair if we don't have hope, which is why Allah (swt) does not remind us of our limits without reminding us that he is capable of everything, and all we have to do is call on Him.

What a mercy that is!

Exercise: Know Thyself

We are limited in every way compared to our Lord. Focus on your personal limita-tions or weaknesses. You can compare the weaknesses to God's abilities (e.g., He knows the future and you do not), or just write down weaknesses you have that you can work on improving (e.g., lack of patience).

MY LIMITATIONS OR WEAKNESSES	HOW I CAN IMPROVE (IF POSSIBLE)

Acknowledge Allah's (swt) Divine Knowledge

If we accepted our limits without believing that there has to be someone or something that has *more* power, *more* knowledge than us, then we would be completely hopeless and depressed. We would be consumed by fear and despair. No one would want to live if there wasn't hope for better or hope for help. This is why we need to acknowledge that there is someone who knows everything we don't, someone we can rely on. Because coming to Islam and staying in the state of Islam means that our religion, our God, gives us hope and fills all the voids we have within ourselves.

One of Allah's (swt) 99 names is Al-Aleem, the All-Knower.

Trusting Allah's (swt) plan means you acknowledge that Allah (swt) is indeed Al-Aleem. You realize that Allah (swt) has divine power and divine ability to know the past, the present, and the future. It's to acknowledge that He knows and you know not. He is the Creator and you are the creation. He is the Master and you are the slave. He is the One and you are the many. He has the solution and you have the problem.

Tawakkul goes back to understanding that we have limited knowledge and Allah (swt) is the All-Knower, so even in a seemingly "bad" situation, we know and trust Allah (swt) will make it the best outcome for us, as long as we believe in Him.

There are multiple instances and stories in the Holy Quran when prophets called out to Allah (swt) in complete trust. The stories of the prophets aren't just stories; they are roadmaps for us to navigate our own lives, our own struggles, and how we can find success just like those who found success before us. They also give us solace, that if God's chosen prophets didn't have all the answers, it's perfectly understandable that we don't either.

Allah (swt) told us about the story of Prophet Nuh (as) (Noah):

۹ ۞ كَذَّبَتْ قَبْلَهُمْ قَوْمُ نُوحٍ فَكَذَّبُوا عَبْدَنَا وَقَالُوا مَجْنُونٌ وَازْدُجِرَ

"Before them, the people of Noah denied the truth and rejected Our servant, calling him insane. And he was intimidated." (Quran 54:9)

In the Quran, Allah (swt) tells us that Prophet Nuh (as) (Noah) called his people to Islam for 950 years. He faced a lot of hardship and even torture, but the people, including his own family, did not follow Prophet Nuh's (as) call to believe in Allah (swt).

My ongoing battle with my kids is that they don't pick up their plates from the dinner table. All they have to do is put them in the sink, but for some reason they are always in such a hurry to run to the next activity that they often forget, and I have to call them back. If they blatantly ignored all of my calls even for a minute, I would be so frustrated and angry, even though my request isn't that serious. But being ignored, especially when you're in the position of care and authority, can feel unbearable and even demeaning.

Now imagine calling people you care for to the correct way of life for 950 years and not only being ignored but being met with intimidation and threats instead.

Subhanallah! How heartbreaking.

فَدَعَا رَبَّهُ أَنِّى مَغْلُوبٌ فَٱنتَصِرْ ١٠

"So he cried out to his Lord, 'I am helpless, so help me!'" (Quran 54:10)

We learn in this verse that even while he was upset, Prophet Nuh (as) did not lose faith in Allah (swt). In his lowest moment, he acknowledged that only Allah (swt) has the power to help him and guide him. He didn't say, "Allah gave me an impossible task!" or "Why me?" as we often do in difficult situations. He did not lose hope in Allah (swt) and he did not blame Him. In fact, he trusted Allah's (swt) plan.

It is human to feel upset or intimidated when people are trying to harm you or when things are not going the way you want, so long as we seek Allah (swt) to help us and acknowledge that He is the only one who can.

Crying out to Allah (swt) for help is the most basic and human way we acknowledge Allah's (swt) divine power and his ability to aid us when no one else can—not even ourselves.

Personal Efforts

"Tie your camel."

This is something every Muslim has heard in their life. According to a *hadith* (a tradition of the Prophet [pbuh]) narrated by Al-Tirmidhi, a man was leaving his home without tying his camel. When he was asked why, he said, "I put my trust in Allah."

But the Prophet (pbuh) told him to tie his camel *and* put his trust in Allah (swt). Side note: Pbuh stands for "peace and blessings upon him," which is the term we say after mentioning the Prophet Muhammad. The Arabic term *sallallahu 'alayhi wa sallam* (saw) can also be used.

There are many variations of this story, but the lesson is the same: we cannot expect the best outcome without putting in our own efforts as well. Both things are required.

Some people will try to use tawakkul as a means of being lazy, manipulative, or just not putting in effort. If you don't put in the work, how can you expect a good result?

This isn't a foreign concept. Even in life, when we want something to happen, when we want success, money, a relationship, a home, or whatever it may be, we have to put in effort to get those things. You cannot want a successful career but not look for a job or start a business. You cannot want a thriving family but not put in the love, care, and sacrifice it takes to have a happy and healthy family and home. You cannot want to get 100 percent on your exam but not study, go to class, nor put in efforts yourself. Just praying before the exam paper will not get you that 100.

You also can't expect people to help you if you're not helping yourself. At first, people will try to lend a hand to someone who needs something, but once they see that that person isn't doing anything for himself, they will stop. Have you ever had someone ask you for help but do nothing themselves? It's infuriating.

I love matchmaking. Sometimes I can see two people who would just be amazing together, and I think trying to help someone get married without wanting anything in return is truly helpful. So I've had a lot of people in my life, friends and acquaintances, who've asked me if I know anybody looking to get married or someone who might be a good match for them. I truly take time to think of someone who might be a good match. But so many times, people will approach me for help but never put in the work themselves. As anyone knows, a matchmaker needs, at the very least, a "biodata." Now, we love laughing at this term but really it's just like a profile on a dating app. I ask for a couple of photos and just some basic information. But I've had so many people who refuse to give me the bare minimum information that I can share. It can get very frustrating running after them when they are the ones who asked for help in the first place. The truth is, if they truly were interested in marriage, they would do their part too. And with those people, I end up not looking anymore.

What's more is if they came back a few months later asking again, I wouldn't take them seriously this time around. Because if I don't see the initiative in the first place, I just don't want to waste my time with someone who isn't serious.

Exercise: Tie Your Camel, Please!

Can you think of a time when someone asked you for help, but you felt they didn't 'tie their camel?' Was there a time you've felt used for help or put in a position where you had to stop helping someone because of the lack of effort from their end? What was that situation? How did it make you feel? Did you still help that person? Would you do things differently looking back?

_____

_____

_____

_____

_____

_____

_____

_____

_____

In the Quran, Allah (swt) shares the story of Musa (as) and the much-needed balance of tawakkul and personal effort. When Musa (as) and the Israelites were leaving Egypt and escaping from the tyranny and oppression of Pharaoh, they came to the Red Sea with nowhere to go. With Pharaoh and his army behind them and a huge sea in front of them, Musa (as) and his people were trapped. Musa (as) had tawakkul and believed in his heart that Allah (swt) would provide a way out, which is exactly why Allah (swt) did. But not before Musa (as) was also asked to do something.

In the Quran, Allah (swt) says:

٦٣ فَأَوْحَيْنَا إِلَىٰ مُوسَىٰ أَنِ اضْرِب بِّعَصَاكَ الْبَحْرَ ۖ فَانفَلَقَ فَكَانَ كُلُّ فِرْقٍ كَالطَّوْدِ الْعَظِيمِ

So We inspired Moses: "Strike the sea with your staff," and the sea was split, each part was like a huge mountain. (Quran 26:63)

Musa (as) was told to complete an action, to strike the sea using his staff. Now could Allah (swt) have split the sea without Musa (as) using his staff?

Of course!

Did the staff itself have anything to do with splitting the sea?

Of course not!

Musa (as) could've simply made *dua*, a prayer, to Allah (swt), and the sea could've been split for them to be saved. But it's Allah's (swt) command to Musa (as) to strike the sea that tells us that indeed our Lord does require us to put in effort, whatever it is that we are capable of, because while it is surely Allah (swt) who gets us out of our troubles, we still have to show the initiative, the work, and our sincerity to be willing to do what it takes as well.

How can we expect Allah (swt) to help us when we don't help ourselves as well? How can we expect guidance, a handhold, the best outcome, when we don't show initiative in our own task?

If you want Allah (swt) to grab your hand and lead you, you have to hold your hand out first.

Unwavering Belief in Allah's (swt) Plan

The final step in tawakkul is when you put it all together. I'd say it's the hardest step of all. Because even when we're aware of it all, understand our shortcomings, know Allah (swt) is the Almighty, and try everything we can, it all comes down to the moment when we're facing the storm head on.

In theory, it is easy to say, "I trust in Allah's plan."

You may even believe that you trust in Allah's (swt) plan, but it is when you are in the depths of despair that the theory has to become practical belief. Up until that point, it may all be lip service. We don't know how strong our tawakkul is or if it's even there at all until we are in the middle of our storm and it's time to put our unwavering trust in Allah (swt).

Let's take a few steps back in the story of Musa (as).

Before Allah (swt) commanded Musa (as) to strike his staff to split the sea, Musa (as) and the Israelites faced their biggest hardship: an oppressive army behind them and an uncrossable sea in front of them. For them, this was certainly the point of "no way out," and this is often when people lose hope, which is exactly what the Israelites did.

فَلَمَّا تَرَ ٱءَا ٱلْجَمْعَانِ قَالَ أَصْحَٰبُ مُوسَىٰٓ إِنَّا لَمُدْرَكُونَ ٦١

> When the two groups came face to face, the companions of Moses cried out, "We are overtaken for sure." (Quran 26:61)

However, the one with true tawakkul, Musa (as), did not lose hope. When an average person can lose hope, a true Muslim does not. And so Musa (as) reminded his people of his firm belief in Allah's (swt) plan.

قَالَ كَلَّآ إِنَّ مَعِىَ رَبِّى سَيَهْدِينِ ٦٢

> Moses reassured them, "Absolutely not! My Lord is certainly with me—He will guide me." (Quran 26:62)

The big question is, how was Musa (as) able to practice his tawakkul? How did Musa (as) have unwavering faith? Because if we can understand how he did, then maybe we can do it the same way.

And the answer is almost too simple: by looking past the problem and staring at the solution.

Musa (as) did not focus on the sea nor on the army that was approaching him. He focused instead on Allah (swt). Any problem we have is nothing compared to the one who has the solution. Not only does Allah (swt) have the solution, He *is* the solution. If Allah (swt) created everything in this world, then the hardships we have were also created by Him, and so are the solutions.

Imagine writing an exam and going through the questions. Some questions are easy and some are difficult. But the rule of the exam is this: you are allowed to ask the teacher for the answer anytime you want. Would you not then ask for help? But we become so focused, so enthralled on the question itself, that we forget we're allowed to raise our hand!

In the Quran, Allah (swt) says,

وَقَالَ رَبُّكُمُ ادْعُونِي أَسْتَجِبْ لَكُمْ

"Your Lord has said, 'Call upon me, I will respond to you.'" (40:60)

Our Most Merciful Lord has already promised us the solution. He has made it clear that in this test of life, all we have to do is ask Him for the answer. So next time you're struggling with having faith in Allah's (swt) plan, understand that you're too focused on the problem. All you need to do is take a step back and realize the one with the solution has been there all along—all you have to do is ask.

Chapter Summary Exercise: Never Stop Learning

What is something new I learned from this chapter, either about Islam or myself?

_____

_____

_____

_____

_____

What am I grateful for today?

_____

_____

_____

_____

_____

How did I lean on Allah (swt) today?

_____

_____

_____

_____

_____

Is there anyone I can forgive today? Or is there someone I should reach out to for forgiveness?

_____

_____

_____

_____

_____

Chapter 3

THE PILLARS: IT'S WHAT WE DO

What is a pillar?

When I think about a pillar, I immediately think of those white columns from Roman times that I learned about in high school. I can imagine the ruins we used to see in videos or textbooks, and no matter how much a structure was destroyed, oftentimes, the white columns were the only thing still standing.

And that's what a good pillar really is, isn't it? A strong, reliable block of foundation that can withstand the test of time. Whether literally or figuratively, a pillar is something that supports and helps to hold up an overall structure or system, and the pillars of Islam are no different because they uphold our system of belief and our way of life.

There are five pillars of Islam (more on these on page 43), and they are the fundamental practices of being a Muslim because believing without acting on those beliefs is an incomplete faith.

Light upon Light

Being a Muslim is believing that Islam is a way of life. It's not just a handbook of dos and don'ts, but rather it's the way we choose to live because we believe in *the* higher power. We spoke about the fact that Islam is giving yourself in submission to God.

Now the problem begins because human beings don't necessarily know exactly what to do in order to submit to God. All the other creations know exactly what to do, because they weren't given a choice in the first place. Remember: they don't have free will. The sun knows how to move around the Earth. The Earth knows how to rotate on its axis. The wind knows how to blow. The trees know how to grow. But without being specifically taught, we don't know what to do in order to give ourselves in submission to Allah (swt).

So Allah (swt) sent messengers, prophets, not just to tell us to believe in Him but *how* to believe in Him. The revelations that prophets bring are light, and when that light meets the light of our souls, our fitrah, we are illuminated. That is the concept of light upon light and *that* is when Islam happens.

Another implication of Islam is peace. So when that outer light and inner light meet and you accept the revelation of a prophet, be it Ibrahim (as) (Abraham), Musa (as) (Moses), Eesa (as) (Jesus), or any prophet, you become at peace with everything around you. Think about it, all of creation is already in submission to God. So if, as human beings, we submit to God as well, we will be in harmony with all other creations.

Islam is a means by which peace is attained within the self and within the world. This is why we believe that nothing, no amount of money, luxury, entertainment, drugs, alcohol, fame, or anything else people run after, can give them peace except a faith in God.

Now, don't get me wrong. Of course, having things like money and luxury are amazing, and there is nothing wrong in wanting them and working to attain them. After all, I'd rather be at peace in a mansion than be at peace living in an alley. But it's a reminder that true peace isn't reliant on worldly luxuries; those are simply bonuses and can sometimes even become distractions that take us away from God.

Exercise: Am I Distracted?

Think about luxuries and bonuses you have in your life. How did your life change for the better once you obtained those luxuries, and how did they cause distractions in your worship or remembrance of Allah (swt)?

LUXURY	BENEFIT	DISTRACTION

The Pillars

The truth is that Allah (swt) has blessed you and chosen you. Allah (swt) has penetrated your heart with His light, and if you accept it and let it meet your inner light, you will ultimately be at peace. After this peace is attained, you are given guidance in concrete actions to follow. The stronger your faith, the easier it will be to strengthen your pillars, which in turn leads to *bushra*, good news, in this Earthly world, and the ultimate good news in the afterlife: Heaven.

Following the pillars of Islam is not always for the faint of heart. Remember, it's often rules and guidelines that make people *not* want to follow a religion. So it's important to understand for yourself the inclination you have to follow this way of life, whether you are on it for the first time or you are renewing your faith.

The five pillars of Islam are:

The Five Pillars of Islam

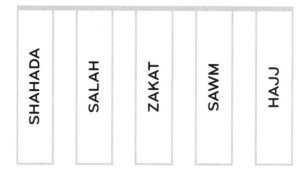

SHAHADA   SALAH   ZAKAT   SAWM   HAJJ

Pillar 1 | Shahada: A Testimony of Faith

The *shahada* is the first and most important pillar of Islam. Think of the shahada as a slogan, or saying, that represents the absolute core belief of the *deen*, the religion. Without this core belief, you cannot be a Muslim.

Ash-hadu An lā 'ilāha 'illā-Allāh wa Ash-hadu An muḥammadun rasūlu-Allāh

"I testify that there is no God but Allah, and Muhammad is the messenger of Allah."

Now what if a non-Muslim just read the *shahada?* Did I trick them into becoming a Muslim? Is this a "gotcha!" moment?

Of course not.

Simply *saying* or reading the shahada isn't enough. You have to sincerely mean it in your heart and accept Islam as your faith. It is light on the tongue but heavy on the scale.

The divinity of the testimony of faith is in the beautiful way it's designed, not just in words and meaning but also in the fact that it's a guide because it teaches us *how* to believe. It teaches us to first empty the vessel we call our heart and fill it with Allah (swt). Whether we believe it or not, we are all worshiping other things or people because there are things in our life that we care and worry about more than God. Some worship money, some fashion, some power, some success, some their children, some their spouse, and some even themselves. So the shahada teaches us that we need to empty our heart of all that we worship before we can worship Allah (swt). When we say *la ilaha* we are declaring there is no one and nothing worthy of worship. We are emptying all things from our heart first then we fill it with *ilallah*, only Allah (swt). If we tried to fill our hearts with Allah (swt) without emptying the vessel first, there wouldn't be any space for Him.

The *shahada* is also what fundamentally separates us from Christianity and Judaism. Because we believe in the same God essentially and the same prophets, like Ibrahim (as), Musa (as), and Eesa (as), this testimony defines that our final messenger who was sent down was Muhammad (pbuh) and the final word of God is the Holy Quran, which was revealed to the Prophet (pbuh).

According to an authentic hadith, the Prophet (pbuh) said, "He whose last words are 'there is no God but Allah,' will enter Paradise."

I don't remember where I first learned this hadith, but for as long as I can remember, I've made it a point to make sure that *lā 'ilāha 'illā-Allāh* is the last thing I say before going to sleep. This way, if I die, my last words will have been a declaration to my Lord and *inshallah*, God willing, I can enter paradise.

Ironically, I used to practice saying the shahada when I was younger so they would be my last words no matter how I died—maybe a car accident or in the hospital. But what I learned as I grew older is what you are used to doing and saying in your lifestyle is what you will think about as you die. So if we are not living a life that is true to our Lord, it will be impossible to worship Him as we die.

Think about what gets "stuck in your head" sometimes. No matter how much you try, you can't get it out. For many people, it could be a song. For people who play games, it might be a sound or saying they often hear. For people who live their life remembering Allah (swt), it will be remembrance of Allah (swt). It's not something you can plan. It will be an unconscious decision your mind and tongue will make based on what they are used to.

Are you thinking about Allah (swt) in your day-to-day life, or is your mind occupied with something or someone else? Truly believing in the shahada isn't just saying it with our lips; it's living it with our actions.

Exercise: Top of the List

Think about your priorities and what you might "worship," then answer the following prompt:

What is most important to me in my life? What would I be lost without if God decided to take it away from me? (It might be a person, money, youth, health, but whatever it is, it's important to understand why it's important to you and how you can work on replacing your attachment with Allah (swt) instead.)

_____

_____

_____

_____

_____

_____

Pillar 2 Salah: The Five Daily Prayers

The most important thing to know about *salah* is that it is a direct link between you, the believer, and Allah (swt). It is your lifeline.

As Muslims, we are extremely blessed that there is no one in between us and our Lord. We do not require someone to pass along our messages, our prayers, our hopes, or our regrets to Allah (swt). There is no worry about anything being lost in translation.

We don't need an *imam*, the person who leads prayers, or anyone else to speak on our behalf.

You get to speak to God, the Master of the Universe, directly, and *that* is a very big deal.

It's like having direct access to the CEO of Apple or Google or some other big company. You don't have to go through the ladder of people to reach out to the man who is running the company. What we would do to get a few moments with Elon Musk or advice from Jeff Bezos. People wait in line for hours, sometimes days, and spend thousands of dollars just to see a celebrity from across the room, and here we are with a direct line to talk to the Creator who can literally make anything happen, and we don't cherish that access nor do we truly use that opportunity.

Salah is often seen as a burden, something that has to be done, boxes that have to be checked, but if we just change our perspective and see it as a privilege, it could change our lives. It is something I love about Islam: I don't need anyone to relay my messages. I don't need to get permission or make an appointment. I talk to my Lord directly and He listens to what I have to say. He has promised me, if I ask, He will provide.

When I was younger, I used to love the Catholic concept of confession. I'm sure it has a lot to do with watching the movies where people go to church and confess their sins to the priest and then they come out feeling at peace with what they are about to do next. I always wanted to say, "Forgive me, Father, for I have sinned..."

As a child and even a teenager, that seemed really cool. But once I got older, I realized our religion already has that, except better because I don't need to confess to anyone but God. And I have a direct link with him through prayer. Because what the movies also showed, was sometimes the person on the other side of the confessional wasn't always sincere or who they pretended to be, but we will never have that problem as Muslims. Confessing to our sins and asking for forgiveness from our Merciful Lord will never be used against us.

Now, I'm not going to lie, it is a little tough to pray five times a day for me personally because, you know, life gets in the way and there are always a million things to do. But that's kind of the point of our salah.

Life is so busy and we are running around trying to get everything done, and in the craziness of it all, it can be easy to forget God. It can be easy to go a little crazy and lose patience and burn out. The point of praying five times a day is to stop everything you are doing, be it work, sleep, or whatever else, and just remember God. It is to remember that we are here on this Earth and are able to do all of these things because God has allowed it and has blessed us with family, friends, work, and life. So, if you take a few minutes a day to remember God and be grateful to Him, it keeps you grounded.

And even though it can get tough to perform all five prayers (I'm not going to pretend it's easy), I do try. And yes, sometimes I miss prayers, or sleep through them, but God is All-Forgiving and Merciful. The important thing is to try your best.

The Five Prayers

1. *Fajr (The Morning Prayer):* This prayer has to be done before sunrise. There is about an hour-and-a-half timespan before sunrise to complete this prayer. And let's be honest, this is usually the hardest prayer for most Muslims. I know it is for me. Personally, it's a little bit easier to pray fajr during the winter months, when sunrise is around 8:00 a.m., and if my kids haven't woken me up by 8, then there is something seriously wrong and I'll probably need all the prayers I can get at that point. But it can be super hard in the summer, when you have to set an alarm for 4:00 in the morning. Sleeping is more convenient than prayer, but we also know prayer is better and more beneficial than sleep.

2. *Dhuhr (The Midday Prayer):* This prayer usually starts around noon, or when the sun is at its highest point in the sky, and you have until the next prayer time starts to pray this prayer, so I find that dhuhr is usually one that is easier for me to pray because there is a long window to pray it.

3. Asr (The Afternoon Prayer): Asr starts immediately after dhuhr, and you can pray it up until about 15 minutes before the next prayer.

4. Maghrib (The Sunset Prayer): This prayer is my favorite, I think. It might be because I love sunsets, as clichéd as that sounds. It starts when the sun starts to set, and it's especially good to pray this prayer on time because there is often a short window before the next prayer.

5. Isha (The Night Prayer): This is the final prayer of the day. You basically have all night to read it, up until the next prayer, which is Fajr. I've found that procrastinating to do this prayer just makes it harder as it gets later. If you don't pray right away, then you can get so tired and sleepy that you get too lazy to pray. But at least you know you have a lot of time for this final prayer.

There are four types of prayers:

Fard: These are the obligatory prayers that are sinful to miss.

Sunnah: These are the prayers the Prophet (pbuh) offered in addition to the obligatory prayers. They are beneficial and encouraged to perform but not sinful to miss.

Wajib: These are necessary prayers.

Nafl: These are optional prayers to reap extra benefits and rewards and can be prayed almost anytime. There is no specific time or amount for them.

There are a certain number of *rakat*, a single group of prescribed movements and verses, you are supposed to perform for each *salah*.

How to Pray

SALAH	FARD	SUNNAH	WAJIB
Fajr	2	2 before fard	None
Dhuhr	4	4 before fard, 2 after fard	None
Asr	4	4 before fard	None
Maghrib	3	2 after fard	None

How to Pray

SALAH	FARD	SUNNAH	WAJIB
Isha	4	4 before fard, 2 after fard	Odd number (1, 3, 5, etc.) of rakats, called witr, at the end

The First Step of Salah

The first step when performing salah starts before the ritual itself. It starts with washing up and making sure you are clean and pure for your meeting with Allah (swt). Just like we wouldn't show up to an important event or meeting dirty or with stinky breath, we must remember, salah is the most important meeting of all and it deserves its proper preparation.

Allah (swt) did not leave us to guess the best way to attend this meeting. Our Merciful Lord tells us how to prepare to meet Him, which starts with making *wudhu*, or ablution. Wudhu is a necessary step to make sure your salah is accepted. Not only is it essential, but it is also an act of worship itself and you get good deeds for making wudhu.

So how do you perform wudhu?

Step 1: Start with the name of Allah (swt) and say, "Bismillah."

Step 2: Wash your hands to your wrists three times.

Step 3: Rinse your mouth and nose three times.

Step 4: Wash your face three times, hairline to chin, ear to ear.

Step 5: Wash your arms, from fingertips to elbows, three times.

Step 6: Wipe your head, from hairline to the nape of the neck, once.

Step 7: Wipe your ears by putting your index fingers in your ears and using your thumb to wipe the back once.

Step 8: Wash your feet up to your ankles, making sure you get water between the toes.

Be sure not to waste water because we are not supposed to be wasteful. Being a Muslim isn't just about rituals and dos and don'ts but also about being a practical and honorable human being with good character. And don't forget, making wudhu wipes away your minor sins, so not only are you getting a reward, but your sins are also literally being washed away with each step. Wudhu doesn't only purify your prayer, it purifies you as well!

Exercise: Time to Pray

Now that you've made wudhu, it's time to pray. While it's most beneficial to pray in a quiet and clean space, sometimes you may not have that option. Maybe you're traveling or outside somewhere. No matter where you are, find a safe space where you can perform your salah and worship your Lord.

There are modesty requirements for salah as well. Men have to be covered from their navel to their knees, but it is highly encouraged for them to have their shoulders covered as well. Women must be covered fully, including their hair, with only their face, their hands, and according to Imam Abu-Hanifah (one of the four scholars), the front of the feet showing.

So, how do you pray?

Salah Steps[1]

Step 1: Stand facing the *qiblah*, the direction of the Holy Kaaba in Mecca.

Step 2: Make an intention for the salah you are praying (e.g., Fajr).

Step 3: Raise your hands to your ears and say "Allahu Akbar," which means "Allah is the Greatest." This is the start of the actual prayer and, until you are done, you cannot talk, smile, or look around. You must focus on the prayer completely.

Step 4: Place your hands on your chest, with your right hand on top of your left hand, look downward, and recite:

---

1 Islamic Association of Raleigh, "How to Perform Salah," last updated September 7, 2021, https://raleighmasjid.org/how-to-perform-salah.

TRANSLITERATION	ARABIC	TRANSLATION
"Subhanaka allahumma wa bi hamdika wa tabara kasmuka wa ta'ala jadduka wa la ilaha ghairuka."	سُبْحَانَكَ اللّٰهُمَّ وَبِحَمْدِكَ، وَتَبَارَكَ اسْمُكَ، وَتَعَالٰى جَدُّكَ، وَلَا إِلٰهَ غَيْرُكَ	"O Allah, how perfect You are and praise be to You. Blessed is Your name, and exalted is Your majesty. There is no god but You."

Step 5: With your hands in the same position, recite:

TRANSLITERATION	ARABIC	TRANSLATION
"A'udhu billahi minash shaitanir rajim. Bismillahir rahmanir rahim."	اعوذ بالله من الشيطان الرجيم بسم الله الرحمن الرحيم	"I seek shelter in Allah from the rejected Satan. In the name of Allah, the most Gracious, the most Merciful."

Step 6: With your hands in the same position, recite the first chapter of the Holy Quran, Surah al-Fatihah:

TRANSLITERATION	ARABIC	TRANSLATION
"Al hamdu lil lahi rabbil 'alamin. Arrahmanir rahim. Maliki yawmiddin. Iyyaka na'budu wa iyyaka nasta'in. Ihdinas siratal mustaqim. Siratal ladhina an'amta'alaihim, ghairil maghdubi'alaihim wa lad dhallin. Ameen."	اَلْحَمْدُ لِلّٰهِ رَبِّ الْعَالَمِيْنَ (١) الرَّحْمٰنِ الرَّحِيْمِ (٢) مٰلِكِ يَوْمِ الدِّيْنِ (٣) اِيَّاكَ نَعْبُدُ وَ اِيَّاكَ نَسْتَعِيْنُ (٤) اِهْدِنَا الصِّرَاطَ الْمُسْتَقِيْمَ (٥) صِرَاطَ الَّذِيْنَ اَنْعَمْتَ عَلَيْهِمْ غَيْرِ الْمَغْضُوْبِ عَلَيْهِمْ وَ لَا الضَّالِّيْنَ (٧)	"All praises and thanks be to Allah, the Lord of the worlds, the most Gracious, the most Merciful, Master of the Day of Judgment. You alone we worship, from You alone we seek help. Guide us along the straight path—the path of those whom You favored, not of those who earned Your anger or went astray."

Step 7: With your hands in the same position, recite any chapter of the Holy Quran. Most often, beginners recite Surah Ikhlas.

TRANSLITERATION	ARABIC	TRANSLATION
"Qul hu wal lahu ahad, allahus samad, lam yalid wa lam yulad, wa lam ya kul lahu kufuwan ahad."	قل هو الله احد،الله الصمد، لم يلد و لم يولد، و لم يكن له كفـوا احد	"Say, He is Allah, the One. Allah is Eternal and Absolute. He begets not, nor was He begotten. And there is none co-equal unto Him."

Step 8: Say "Allahu Akbar" and bow down while placing our hands on your knees. This position is called rukoo. Recite "Subhana Rabbiyal Adhim" three times. This means "How perfect is my Lord, the Supreme."

Step 9: Stand up from the bowing position while saying "Sami'Allahu liman hamidah," meaning "Allah hears those who praise Him." Then say "Rabbana lakal hamd," meaning "Our Lord, praise be to You."

Step 10: Say "Allahu Akbar" and prostrate on the ground with your forehead, nose, the palms of your hands, your knees, and your toes touching the floor. This position is called sujood. With your head on the ground, recite "Subhana Rabbiyal A'la" three times. This means "How perfect is my Lord, the Highest."

Step 11: Sit up from the floor, saying "Allahu Akbar." Place your hands on your knees in the sitting position and say, "Rabbighfir li," meaning "Oh my Lord, forgive me."

Step12: Say "Allahu Akbar" and prostrate on the ground again in sujood. Recite "Subhana Rabbiyal A'la" three times.

Step 13: Say "Allahu Akbar" and get up from this position.

This completes one rakah, or unit of the prayer. Depending on which salah you are praying, you can repeat steps 5 through 13 for the next unit(s). For example, since Fajr has two rakats, you would stand up and repeat these steps one more time to complete both rakats.

Step 14: After the second sujood (prostration), sit up putting more weight on the left leg while keeping the right foot upright. Put your hands on your knees and recite Tashahhud:

TRANSLITERATION	ARABIC	TRANSLATION
At-tahiyyatu lillahi was-salawatu wat-tayyibat, as-salamu 'alaika ayyuhan-Nabiyyu wa rahmatAllahi wa baraktuhu. As-salamu 'alaina wa 'ala 'ibad illahis-salihin, *Lift your right index finger for the following part:* *Ashahdu an la illaha ill-Allah wa ashhadu anna Muhammadan 'abduhu wa rasuluhu*	التّحِيّاتُ لِلّهِ والصّلَواتُ والطّيّبّاتُ السّلامُ عَلَيْكَ أيّها النّبِيّ وَرَحْمَةُ اللّهِ وَبَرَكاتُهُ السّلامُ عَلَيْنا وَعَلى عِبادِ اللّهِ الصّالحِينَ *Lift your right index finger for the following part* أشْهَدُ أنْ لا إلهَ إلّا اللّهُ وأشْهَدُ أنّ مُحَمّدًا عَبْدُهُ وَرَسُولُهُ	All the compliments are for Allah and all the prayers and all the good things (are for Allah). Peace be on you, O Prophet, and Allah's mercy and blessings (are on you). And peace be on us and on the good (pious) worshipers of Allah. *Lift your right index finger for the following part:* I testify that none has the right to be worshiped but Allah and that Muhammad is His slave and Apostle.

For a prayer with 2 rakat, you continue to Step 15 and complete your salah.

For a prayer with 3 rakat, you would now stand up and perform another unit of prayer (steps 5 through 13) and continue until the end of the salah.

For a prayer with 4 rakat, you perform another unit of prayer (steps 5 to 13) for your third rakat. Then stand up again and do your fourth rakat until the end of the salah.

Step 15: Stay seated and recite Assalatul-Ibrahimiyah:

TRANSLITERATION	ARABIC	TRANSLATION
Allahumma salli 'ala Muhammadin wa 'ala aali Muhammad *Kamaa salayta 'ala Ibraaheem wa 'ala aali Ibrahim* *Innaka Hameedun Majeed* *Wa baarik 'ala Muhammadin wa 'ala aali Muhammad* *Kamaa baarakta 'ala Ibraaheem wa 'ala aali Ibrahim* *Innaka Hameedun Majeed*	اللَّهُمَّ صَلِّ عَلَى مُحَمَّدٍ وَعَلَى آلِ مُحَمَّدٍ كَمَا صَلَّيْتَ عَلَى إِبْرَاهِيمَ وَعَلَى آلِ إِبْرَاهِيمَ إِنَّكَ حَمِيدٌ مَّجِيدٌ اللَّهُمَّ بَارِكْ عَلَى مُحَمَّدٍ وَعَلَى آلِ مُحَمَّدٍ كَمَا بَارَكْتَ عَلَى إِبْرَاهِيمَ وَعَلَى آلِ إِبْرَاهِيمَ إِنَّكَ حَمِيدٌ مَّجِيدٌ	"O Allah, let Your mercy come upon Muhammad and the family of Muhammad as You let it come upon Ibrahim and the family of Ibrahim. O Allah, bless Muhammad and the family of Muhammad as You blessed Ibrahim and the family of Ibrahim. Truly You are Praiseworthy and Glorious."

Step 16: To complete the salah, turn your face to the right shoulder and recite, "Assalamu alaikum wa rahmatullah," then turn your face to the left shoulder and recite again, "Assalamu alaikum wa rahmatullah." This means "peace and the mercy of Allah be on you."

You have now completed your salah and this is a great opportunity to make dua, supplicate, and ask Allah (swt) for whatever your heart desires. May He ease for you your worries and grant you His ultimate peace and blessings. Ameen!

Exercise: Salah Activity

Objective: Earn more points each day than the day before.

Let's start by being accountable for prayer for one week. Complete the calendar according to the point system. Total the points at the end of each day. If there are fewer points on any day than the day before, give $5 of sadaqah, or charity. This way you are receiving a reward regardless.

Point System:

⁂ *Fard = 2 points*   ⁂ *Sunnah = 1 point*

⁂ *Wajib = 2 points*   ⁂ *Nafl = 1 point*

	SUN	MON	TUES	WED	THURS	FRI	SAT
FAFR	☐	☐	☐	☐	☐	☐	☐
DHUHR	☐	☐	☐	☐	☐	☐	☐
ASR	☐	☐	☐	☐	☐	☐	☐
MAGHRIB	☐	☐	☐	☐	☐	☐	☐
ISHA	☐	☐	☐	☐	☐	☐	☐
TOTAL (POINTS)							
SADAQAH ($)							

Tips:

1. If you missed a prayer, make it up. It is always better to do a prayer late than not at all!

2. Sunnah prayer is always a good way to get an extra reward.

3. If you are unable to pray (due to menstruating, illness, etc.) and it's the time for prayer, you still make wudhu and sit and do dhikr, praise and remember God, for a few minutes. That way your day is still built around setting aside time for Allah (swt), and this helps to sustain a routine for every day.

Feed Your Soul

What do our bodies need to survive? The basic necessities are food and water, and our bodies let us know when it's time to eat or drink. We get signals from our body when it isn't nourished: our stomach may growl, we may feel pain, our throat feels dry. But we know as living, breathing, thinking, feeling human beings we are not only our bodies. There are other equally important parts of us, one being our *ruh*, our soul. Even after we die and lose our earthly body, the essence of us lives on and goes into the *akhirah*, the afterlife. So while it's important that we feed our bodies, it's even more important that we feed the eternal part of us: our souls.

So what is the food of the soul? How do we replenish our souls? How do we feel fulfilled in our essence?

Well, in the Quran, Allah (swt) tells us:

وَمَا خَلَقْتُ ٱلْجِنَّ وَٱلْإِنسَ إِلَّا لِيَعْبُدُونِ ٥٦

"I did not create jinn and humans except to worship me." (Quran 51:56)

Our soul's inclination is to worship Allah (swt) alone, and it is how we feed our souls. Without it, we feel empty, lost, and never satisfied. If we don't worship Allah (swt), no matter how much "good" we seemingly have, no matter what we do to enjoy ourselves and fulfill ourselves, it will fall short. When you are starving, it doesn't matter if you watch your favorite TV show or spend time with the ones you love most in the world or buy the most amazing car. None of those things will satisfy your hunger, and without food you will feel sick, empty, and eventually die. So if we're not worshiping Allah (swt), none of the seemingly happy things in life will fulfill us.

And the best, most necessary, and commanded way of worshiping Allah (swt) is by performing salah.

Salah is your connection to your Lord, the food of your soul and the purpose of your being.

To Pray or Not to Pray

Obviously, the answer is always to pray. But the truth is, when you're not in the habit of praying, it can be tough to start and stay consistent with praying five times a day, especially as our *iman*, our faith, goes up and down. There may be times where we are super motivated to pray and times when praying is the hardest thing in the world.

So what can you do to help stay on track with your prayers? Here are a few tips and tricks that can help:

- ✳ **Realize the importance of prayer in the first place.** According to a hadith of the Prophet (pbuh), the first thing we will be questioned about on the Day of Judgment is our salah. If you're given an exam and you're told the first question and how much it's worth, wouldn't you prepare for it? There is no question about the importance of what salah is, so give it its due respect.

- ✳ **Realize prayer is a privilege, not a burden.** Change the way you think about your salah. Instead of thinking you *have* to pray, think that you *can* pray. Remember what we discussed earlier, salah is the privilege of having direct access to the Creator, the founder of the universe.

- ✳ **Always have wudhu.** I find wudhu to be the hardest part of prayer. If I have my wudhu I can get up and pray without effort, but if I have to go and wash up first, I feel lazy and may even end up delaying my salah. My best-kept secret to salah is that I almost always have wudhu. I wake up in the morning and make wudhu as part of my morning routine, whether I am praying immediately or not. If I use the bathroom at any point in the day, I make wudhu after washing my hands. This way, no matter the time of day, I am always prepared for salah.

- ✳ **Set your intention to pray five times a day, no matter what.** I recently watched a video by a content creator named Subhi Taha, and he shared his tip for getting into the habit of prayer. Start by praying five times a day no matter what, whether it's late or on time—pray! Even if you were out all day and end up praying all the prayers back-to-back before bed, do it! Of course the goal is to pray on time every day but start where you can because sometimes when you miss one salah, you might miss another, and by the end of the day, you haven't prayed at all and the next day the cycle repeats. Before you know it, it's been a week, a month, maybe even a year since you've prayed. Praying five times a day no matter what will help you stay on the path, even if it isn't perfect.

- ✳ **Plan your day around salah.** Instead of trying to fit salah into your busy schedule, try to plan your day around salah, instead. This may seem difficult, but anytime you set your intention and plan for good, Allah (swt) makes it easy for us to follow through.

Exercise: My Day around Salah

Think about your average day. What are you normally doing at the time of prayers? Write down where you are, what you do, and if you can easily access your salah at that time. If not, what can you do to make things easier to pray on time?

SALAH	DAILY ROUTINE
Fajr	
Dhuhr	
Asr	
Maghrib	
Isha	

Pillar 3 | Zakat: Charity

If you Google *zakat*, you might be told by the wonderful internet that it translates to almsgiving. Now, I know what you're thinking because I was thinking the same thing:

What the heck is almsgiving? Is that even an English word?

Well, apparently it is.

So to save you time I Googled almsgiving for the both of us and it means giving money, food, or other materials to the poor; i.e., charity.

So what is the difference between *sadaqah*, general charity, and zakat? Sadaqah doesn't really have any rules attached to it. You can give this form of charity whenever and to whomever you please. As a matter of fact, just smiling at someone is a form of sadaqah.

Zakat, on the other hand, is also a form of charity, but it has specific rules attached to it. For example, zakat is to be given once a year and the amount you give depends on how much money or gold you have. There are also only specific people who can receive zakat; you can't just give it to anyone.

In general, the amount of zakat that should be given a year depends on your financial assets and savings that are not used toward your living expenses; 2.5 percent of those savings should be donated. Zakat is a way for us to purify our wealth and to help provide for those who are less fortunate. There is a special blessing in giving charity for the sake of Allah (swt). It is never a loss of wealth and in fact multiplies the blessings in our lives in ways we can't imagine.

In the Quran, Allah (swt) tells us:

وَأَقِيمُوا الصَّلَاةَ وَآتُوا الزَّكَاةَ وَأَقْرِضُوا اللَّهَ قَرْضًا حَسَنًا ۚ وَمَا تُقَدِّمُوا لِأَنفُسِكُم مِّنْ خَيْرٍ تَجِدُوهُ
عِندَ اللَّهِ هُوَ خَيْرًا وَأَعْظَمَ أَجْرًا ۚ وَاسْتَغْفِرُوا اللَّهَ ۖ إِنَّ اللَّهَ غَفُورٌ رَّحِيمٌ

"...and establish Prayer, and pay Zakah, and give Allah a goodly loan. Whatever good you send forth for yourselves, you shall find it with Allah. That is better and its reward is greater. And ask for Allah's forgiveness; surely He is Most Forgiving, Most Compassionate." (Quran 73:20)

Allah (swt) tells us giving zakat is like giving a loan to Allah (swt) himself and it is He, the Lord of the worlds who will pay you back exponentially. Zakat is mentioned in the Holy Quran 30 times (or so) and it is encouraged to give in charity as a benefit to us.

- ❊ If you're in a hardship: give charity.
- ❊ If you want more money: give charity.
- ❊ If you need help: give charity.
- ❊ If you need guidance: give charity.
- ❊ If you want to get married: give charity.
- ❊ If you want forgiveness: give charity.
- ❊ If you want to have kids: give charity.

Charity seems like an apparent loss—literally you are giving money away—but when you have true tawakkul and trust in Allah's (swt) words and promises, that charity is multiplied and given to us and our children in ways we don't even know, through provisions we never imagined. So never feel like you are facing a loss in giving charity and helping those in need. Give with a smile on your face because you truly believe that the Provider will provide.

Pillar 4 Sawm: Fasting

Sawm is fasting in the month of Ramadan, the holiest month in the Islamic calendar. Our fasts start at dawn, before fajr, and end at sunset, at *maghrib*. Fasting in the month of Ramadan isn't just about abstaining from eating while the sun is out, but also practicing abstaining from all vices and bad habits such as gluttony, bad language, and fighting. It's the month when you literally try to be the best person you can be.

So why do we fast?

A common misconception is that we fast to feel the hunger that poor people feel, but that's not actually the reason, though it does help us to understand our blessings. We fast, as we do anything else, because it is a command from our Lord. It's important to remember this because sometimes we try to rationalize and justify obligations. While there are always benefits to every obligation, the first and foremost reason we should do anything is to please Allah (swt), whether we fully understand the benefit or not.

In the Quran, Allah (swt) says,

يَـٰٓأَيُّهَا ٱلَّذِينَ ءَامَنُوا۟ كُتِبَ عَلَيْكُمُ ٱلصِّيَامُ كَمَا كُتِبَ عَلَى ٱلَّذِينَ مِن قَبْلِكُمْ لَعَلَّكُمْ تَتَّقُونَ

"O you who believe! Observing As-Sawm (the fasting) is prescribed for you
as it was prescribed for those before you, that you may become Al-Muttaqun
(pious)." (Quran 2:183)

Al-Muttaqun are those who have *taqwa*. Taqwa is often translated as God-consciousness, or fearing God. However, while it is necessary to fear Allah (swt), sometimes the word "fear" is manipulated to show God in a negative light. Having taqwa is not necessarily about being afraid of God; rather, it is about having a deep respect and love for Him, and striving to live in a way that is pleasing to Him—much like children who respect their parents and fear disappointing them.

Taqwa is also a means of protection, because if we are truly mindful of Allah's (swt) Greatness and abilities, we are more likely to avoid actions that could lead to harm or negative consequences.

I remember I was fasting one day in high school, and a girl in my class offered me food. After I told her I couldn't eat since I was fasting, she said something I'll never forget:

"Just eat. It's not like anyone will know. Your parents aren't here."

I remember thinking how absurd that was—as if I was fasting for my parents or my Islamic values would change based on who was around me. I almost felt sorry for her. She didn't understand that fasting wasn't for my parents or other people. Fasting was for God. He would know. He knows all. He sees all and I would be so disappointed if He were disappointed in me.

This is one of the ways fasting helps us gain taqwa.

There are other reasons to fast as well. It teaches us to be patient, to have control over our wants and needs. It teaches us resilience. It teaches us to be closer to God and always be conscious of God. It teaches us to be thankful because there are people in this world who literally have no food. There are people who live in countries ravaged by war and famine. Fasting is just a month of restraint for us, and we still get food at the end of the day, but for some people, fasting is life. There are even people who fast in the month of Ramadan and don't have food to break their fast with. It really puts into perspective all the things that God has blessed us with.

Fasting also teaches us that we can have a life and a satisfaction for life outside of eating and drinking and fulfilling our bodily needs. It's in this month of fasting that we worry more about feeding our soul. Not eating or drinking for one day helps you realize how much time there really is in the day. Sometimes it feels like the day will never end. And when we have so much more free time not worrying about where we are going to eat or what we are going to cook, we have more time to reflect, to meditate and pray to God. We feel more spiritual happiness and fulfillment in this month than we do all year round because our soul's needs become more important than our body's needs.

What's more is Allah (swt) is so merciful that He has made fasting for those who can handle it and are capable of it. Children don't have to fast. The sick don't have to fast, whether you are sick for a few days, or if you have a chronic illness or condition that doesn't allow you to fast at all. When a woman is on her period, she's not supposed to fast. If you start feeling sick or something comes up that you can no longer fast, you are allowed to break your fast. If you are traveling, you don't have to fast. If you are pregnant or breastfeeding, you don't have to fast. The list goes on. Allah (swt) is not punishing us or torturing us. He is healing us in ways we don't even understand, and He is giving us the much-needed time to feed our souls, which end up getting neglected throughout the year.

Once I was fasting and I totally forgot (thank you, pregnancy and children for making me lose brain cells), so I ate french fries. And not just any french fries—homemade fries that I sprinkled with *chaat masala* (a savory South Asian spice that makes everything taste amazing), and I enjoyed every little bite. Only after I finished eating them, I realized I was fasting!

Did that break my fast?

No! It certainly did not because Allah's (swt) mercy is vast and when we do things by accident because we are human after all, Allah (swt) does not punish us for our short-comings. In fact, my forgetfulness and those fries were considered a gift from God and I got to continue fasting for the rest of the day.

How merciful is Our Creator!

Exercise: Ready. Set. Fast!

Keep track of your fasts!

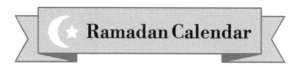

Ramadan Calendar

DAY	FAJR	MAGHRIB	FASTED
1	Yes ❑ No ❑	Yes ❑ No ❑	Yes ❑ No ❑
2	Yes ❑ No ❑	Yes ❑ No ❑	Yes ❑ No ❑
3	Yes ❑ No ❑	Yes ❑ No ❑	Yes ❑ No ❑
4	Yes ❑ No ❑	Yes ❑ No ❑	Yes ❑ No ❑
5	Yes ❑ No ❑	Yes ❑ No ❑	Yes ❑ No ❑
6	Yes ❑ No ❑	Yes ❑ No ❑	Yes ❑ No ❑
7	Yes ❑ No ❑	Yes ❑ No ❑	Yes ❑ No ❑
8	Yes ❑ No ❑	Yes ❑ No ❑	Yes ❑ No ❑
9	Yes ❑ No ❑	Yes ❑ No ❑	Yes ❑ No ❑
10	Yes ❑ No ❑	Yes ❑ No ❑	Yes ❑ No ❑
11	Yes ❑ No ❑	Yes ❑ No ❑	Yes ❑ No ❑
12	Yes ❑ No ❑	Yes ❑ No ❑	Yes ❑ No ❑
13	Yes ❑ No ❑	Yes ❑ No ❑	Yes ❑ No ❑

DAY	FAJR	MAGHRIB	FASTED
14	Yes ❑ No ❑	Yes ❑ No ❑	Yes ❑ No ❑
15	Yes ❑ No ❑	Yes ❑ No ❑	Yes ❑ No ❑
16	Yes ❑ No ❑	Yes ❑ No ❑	Yes ❑ No ❑
17	Yes ❑ No ❑	Yes ❑ No ❑	Yes ❑ No ❑
18	Yes ❑ No ❑	Yes ❑ No ❑	Yes ❑ No ❑
19	Yes ❑ No ❑	Yes ❑ No ❑	Yes ❑ No ❑
20	Yes ❑ No ❑	Yes ❑ No ❑	Yes ❑ No ❑
21	Yes ❑ No ❑	Yes ❑ No ❑	Yes ❑ No ❑
22	Yes ❑ No ❑	Yes ❑ No ❑	Yes ❑ No ❑
23	Yes ❑ No ❑	Yes ❑ No ❑	Yes ❑ No ❑
24	Yes ❑ No ❑	Yes ❑ No ❑	Yes ❑ No ❑
25	Yes ❑ No ❑	Yes ❑ No ❑	Yes ❑ No ❑
26	Yes ❑ No ❑	Yes ❑ No ❑	Yes ❑ No ❑
27	Yes ❑ No ❑	Yes ❑ No ❑	Yes ❑ No ❑
28	Yes ❑ No ❑	Yes ❑ No ❑	Yes ❑ No ❑
29	Yes ❑ No ❑	Yes ❑ No ❑	Yes ❑ No ❑
30	Yes ❑ No ❑	Yes ❑ No ❑	Yes ❑ No ❑

Pillar 5 Hajj—Pilgrimage

Hajj, the ultimate pilgrimage, is the only pillar of Islam that only needs to be completed once in your life, though of course you are welcome to perform it multiple times. Muslims from all around the world travel to the Holy *Kaaba* in Mecca, Saudi Arabia, in the Islamic month of *Dhul Hijjah.*

As Hasan Minhaj said in his Netflix original show, *Patriot Act,* "It's like Coachella for Muslims except you can't be annoyed when people say they had a really religious experience."

Indeed it is a very religious and humbling experience. We pray, we worship, and we are in our most basic form. During Hajj, especially the ritualistic portions such as circling the Holy Kaaba during *tawaf* or while sleeping under the open sky in *Muzdilfah,* there is no difference between us. We realize we are all the same except in our faith. What someone does for a living or how much money they make or who they are related to doesn't matter.

We are all there simply to worship Allah (swt), the only reason we were created in the first place.

Chapter Summary Exercise: Never Stop Learning

What is something new I learned from this chapter—either about Islam or myself?

_____

_____

_____

_____

_____

_____

What am I grateful for today?

_____

_____

_____

_____

_____

How did I lean on Allah (swt) today?

_____

_____

_____

_____

_____

Is there anyone I can forgive today? Or is there someone I should reach out to for forgiveness?

_____

_____

_____

_____

_____

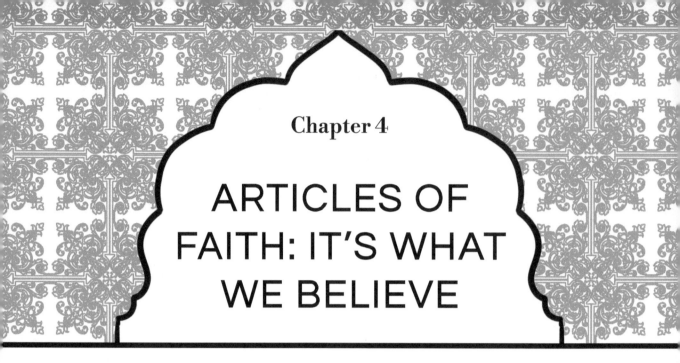

Chapter 4

ARTICLES OF FAITH: IT'S WHAT WE BELIEVE

You are what you believe.

The beginning of our deen starts with our faith. It depends and relies on what we believe in our hearts. Of course, first and foremost that means we believe in the one and only God, Allah (swt). Next, it means we believe that Prophet Muhammad (pbuh) is God's last and final Messenger. But our belief doesn't stop there. Once we believe and take the testimony of our faith, we're also taught what else and who else to believe in, especially when it comes to things that we cannot see with our eyes.

As Muslims, we have six articles of faith. They are our core beliefs about the nature of God, the prophets, and the religion itself.

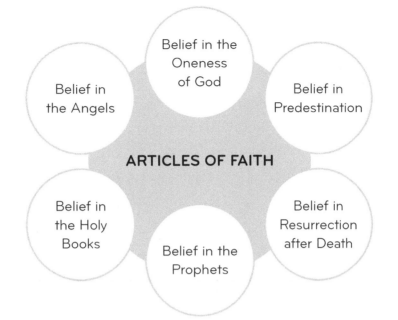

Belief in the Oneness of God

Belief in the Angels

Belief in Predestination

ARTICLES OF FAITH

Belief in the Holy Books

Belief in the Prophets

Belief in Resurrection after Death

Tawhid: Belief in the Oneness of God

Islam is one of the monotheistic religions in its truest form. The most important aspect of understanding Islam and being a Muslim is believing in the oneness of God. This is *tawhid*, and it is often what brings people to Islam. Many people who find their way to the deen do so because they believe in a singular higher power, as many religions have associated partners with God in one way or another.

Allah (swt) reminds us in the Quran,

وَقُلِ ٱلْحَمْدُ لِلَّهِ ٱلَّذِى لَمْ يَتَّخِذْ وَلَدًا وَلَمْ يَكُن لَّهُ شَرِيكٌ فِى ٱلْمُلْكِ وَلَمْ يَكُن لَّهُ وَلِىٌّ مِّنَ ٱلذُّلِّ ۖ وَكَبِّرْهُ تَكْبِيرًا ١١١

"And say, 'Praise to Allah, who has not taken a son and has had no partner in [His] dominion and has no [need of a] protector out of weakness; and glorify Him with [great] glorification.'" (Quran 17:111)

We are not allowed to associate any partner or kin with Allah (swt). Allah (swt) is independent of all things and people. He is the start and the end of all things and requires no help, companionship, or family. Any association with Allah (swt) is *shirk*, which is often considered an unforgivable sin. Even though Allah (swt) is *Ar-Rahmaan* and *Ar-Raheem*, the Most Gracious and the Most Merciful, and loves to forgive us for all things as long as we repent, some scholars say that there are texts that indicate that major shirk can take you outside the fold of Islam. Of course, Allah (swt) is capable of forgiving the sincere repentance of His slaves; this shows the utmost importance of tawhid.

There are two kinds of shirk: major and minor. A major shirk is ascribing any partner or rival to God, and it's very easy to understand if we do that or not. A minor shirk, however, can get a little complicated and is something we have to be very careful about because it's not often something we do on purpose.

Minor shirks can be using objects as protection from the "evil eye" or swearing on something or someone other than Allah (swt). It can be when we "knock on wood" not to jinx something. These types of actions give power to that object or person instead of Allah (swt). Allah (swt) is our Protector, not a blue eye image on a bracelet or a dreamcatcher hanging on our bed.

A Heart Full Of...

There is another form of minor shirk that, for me, is the most dangerous of all: our attachments.

Our attachments are things that we fill our hearts with, things we couldn't live without, and things we love the most in this world, even more than Allah (swt), our Source of Love. They are things that we use to fill ourselves with, but that can never fulfill us. They are often the things that end up breaking our hearts because they were never meant to be in our hearts in the first place.

Yasmin Mogahed explains in her book *Reclaim Your Heart* that anything that we hold in our heart is our attachment, and it is the thing we love the most in this world. For all intents and purposes, it is what we worship because it is what is more important to us. Therefore, Allah (swt) should be in our hearts because He is the only one worthy of worship. Then, when He blesses us with gifts—our families, our looks, our friends, our careers, our education, our children, our parents, our talents, our bodies—we should love them and appreciate them, but never more than Allah (swt). We should hold them in our hands, not our heart.

Our attachment should be to Allah (swt), first and foremost, because those things, those blessings, can be taken away just as fast as they were given to us, and if they are, we should not become hopeless and should still be grateful to Allah (swt).

What ends up happening, however, is we hold the gifts in our hearts, and we hold Allah (swt) in our hands. Many times we are willing to give up or delay worshiping Allah (swt), the Gifter, for the gift. We have it backward.

※ If we are attached to our spouse—we might be tested with divorce.

※ If we are attached to our parents—we might be tested with their deaths.

※ If we are attached to our children—we might be tested with losing them.

※ If we are attached to our careers—we might be tested with losing our job.

※ If we are attached to our body or looks—we might be tested with bodily loss.

All of these tests are possible, and people go through them every day. But these tests should strengthen us in a way that we remember and worship our Lord even more. They should remind us of the fleeting status of this world and that we are not here forever. These tests should bring us closer to Allah (swt) and help us seek Him for strength. But if our attachment is so much stronger than our love of Allah (swt), then we could become hopeless and devastated instead. We could end up hating Allah (swt) or being upset with him, which is the worst punishment of all.

If our attachment is to anything or anyone other than Allah (swt), eventually we will have our hearts broken because nothing lasts forever, other than our Lord.

Exercise: Where Is My Heart?

Prioritize your top five attachments—the things you love the most in this world.

1. _____

2. _____

3. _____

4. _____

5. _____

Be honest with yourself, is your connection with God on that list? Imagine if you lost those blessings. How would your life change? Would you survive? How would you focus on filling your heart with Allah (swt) instead? Or imagine a time you did lose something or someone you love. How did you cope?

_____

_____

_____

_____

_____

_____

_____

_____

Malaikah: Belief in the Angels

It's easy to believe in things we can see, but it's the things we don't that really require faith. This is why believing in angels is an article of faith—because we can't see them. Anything we can't see is considered to be part of the world of *ghayb*, the unseen.

Allah (swt) created the angels before He created human beings to fulfill certain responsibilities, and He tells us about them in the Quran. They are made of light, have a "great size," have wings, and do not eat or drink. Allah (swt) created angels without free will, and they praise Allah (swt) constantly, so they are completely different from mankind. Even though angels do not have free will, when Allah (swt) decided to create mankind, the angels did question Allah's decision.

وَإِذْ قَالَ رَبُّكَ لِلْمَلَـٰٓئِكَةِ إِنِّي جَاعِلٌ فِى ٱلْأَرْضِ خَلِيفَةًۖ قَالُوٓا۟ أَتَجْعَلُ فِيهَا مَن يُفْسِدُ فِيهَا
وَيَسْفِكُ ٱلدِّمَآءَ وَنَحْنُ نُسَبِّحُ بِحَمْدِكَ وَنُقَدِّسُ لَكَۖ قَالَ إِنِّىٓ أَعْلَمُ مَا لَا تَعْلَمُونَ ٣٠

Remember when your Lord said to the angels, "I am going to place a successive human authority on earth." They asked Allah (swt), "Will You place in it someone who will spread corruption there and shed blood while we glorify Your praises and proclaim Your holiness?" Allah (swt) responded, "I know what you do not know." (Quran 2:30)

This is a reminder to us that Allah (swt) does not need us to worship Him and praise Him. There are creations who already do that and if Allah (swt) wanted, He could have created us the same way. Worshiping and praising Allah (swt) does not benefit Allah (swt), it actually benefits us. Allah (swt) is the Almighty, the Creator, the Sustainer, the Lord, whether we say it or not. It is us who need Allah (swt), not the other way around.

There are all sorts of angels, and each has different responsibilities. While we don't know all of the angels and there is a lot that is unknown about them, here are some angels that we do know about.

ANGELS IN ISLAM	DUTIES AND RESPONSIBILITIES
Jibreel	❈ Entrusted with carrying revelation to the Prophets. (Quran 26:192–195) ❈ Allah (swt) has called him *Ruh-ul-Qudus*, known to be the "Holy Spirit." (Quran 2:253)
Mika'el	❈ Provides sustenance; i.e., provides rain to the earth to help plants grow and provides water to the creatures
Azrael	❈ Known as the "Angel of Death" (*Malak-al-Mawt*). ❈ Angel responsible for retrieving the soul from the body at the time of death. (Quran 32:11)
Munkar and Nakir	❈ Angels responsible for questioning the souls in the grave. ❈ Questions everyone will be asked: "Who is your Lord? What is your religion? Who was your Prophet?"
Israfel	❈ Known as "Angel of Soor" (the trumpet). ❈ Responsible for blowing the trumpet on the Day of Judgment. ❈ In the hadith, it is mentioned the trumpet will be blown twice. First, it will occur on the Day of Judgment. Second, it will begin the resurrection of all of Mankind.
The Angels of Kiraman Katibin	❈ These angels are responsible for recording all good and bad deeds. ❈ The angel on the right records good deeds, while the angel on the left records the bad deeds. (Quran 82: 10–12)
The Angels of Muqarrabun	❈ These angels are known to be in constant worship of Allah (swt) by glorifying Him without pause. (Quran 4:172)
Harut and Marut	❈ Angels sent to Prophet Sulaiman (as) to teach and warn him about black magic. (Quran 2:102)

Kutub: Belief in the Holy Books

Most people don't know this, but all of the original holy books of the major monotheistic religions—Judaism, Christianity, and Islam—are in fact Allah's (swt) books. The holy books were revealed by Allah (swt) to the believers of the time and are considered the word of Allah (swt) as long as they are kept in their original form. Unfortunately, none were, other than the Holy Quran, of course.

لَقَدْ اَرْسَلْنَا رُسُلَنَا بِالْبَيِّنَاتِ وَاَنْزَلْنَا مَعَهُمُ الْكِتَابَ وَالْمِيزَانَ لِيَقُومَ النَّاسُ بِالْقِسْطِ

"Indeed We have sent Our Messengers with clear proofs, and revealed with them the Scripture and the Balance (justice) that mankind may keep up justice." (Quran, 57:25)

The holy books are revelations that were sent to certain prophets throughout history. There are four books that are considered to be the most important in Islam:

1. *The Torwat (Torah):* This book was sent to Prophet Musa (as) and is associated with the Jewish faith. However, the original Torah was lost because the book was changed and altered.

2. *The Zabur:* This book of Allah (swt) was revealed to Prophet Dawud (as), also known as David. It means "songs" in Arabic, and the original form has also been lost.

3. *The Injeel (Gospel):* These were the revelations that were revealed to Prophet Eesa (as), Jesus.

4. *The Holy Quran:* This is our Holy Book, and it was revealed to Prophet Muhammad (pbuh) as his miracle. It is the final and complete revelation of Allah's (swt) will and is the source of not just our laws, but our way of life. The Quran has never been altered or changed, and it never will be.

The Greatest Miracle of All Time

ذَٰلِكَ ٱلْكِتَٰبُ لَا رَيْبَ ۛ فِيهِ ۛ هُدًى لِّلْمُتَّقِينَ ٢

"This is the Book! There is no doubt about it—a guide for those mindful of Allah." (Quran 2:2)

This is how Allah (swt) introduces His book to us: it is a guide, and it is the truth—but only for those who have taqwa because those are the people who have truly opened their eyes and hearts. The Quran is divine because it is the word of Allah (swt). It is perfect in every way and it is the guidance we need to live in this world.

The Quran is the greatest miracle of all time. Even though it was revealed to the Prophet (pbuh) over 1,400 years ago, it is just as relevant now as it was back then. The Quran does not lose value, nor does it only apply to one person, time, or place. The Quran can be opened at any page, any line, any word, and it can and will relate to you in every aspect of your life. That is the special thing about the Quran. Even if you don't understand the Quran, just listening to it brings you solace, peace, and healing because of its divinity. The Quran taught us everything about this world. Even before science was able to prove certain concepts, those concepts were already mentioned in the Quran.

So if you're seeking that closeness, that high, that faith, then turn to the words of Allah (swt) and seek solace in His revelations. The Quran is how Allah (swt) speaks with us.

But are we even listening?

I've found that anytime I've been feeling low or lost, it's often because I have lost touch with the Quran. Before you know it, it's been days, weeks, months, maybe even years that have gone by without you reading the Quran. The times in my life that I have consistently read and understood the words of my Lord are when I am actively taking Quran classes, whether it's for learning it for the first time, practicing my recitation, working on my *tajweed* (pronunciation), or memorizing verses or chapters. It's when I have actively had a teacher whom I am held accountable to that I have not let the Quran slip by.

A couple of years ago I restarted the Quran. I wanted to work on my tajweed and make sure I understood the rules, like when to make a certain sound, when to take a breath, when to stop, and so on. And I'm going to be honest, I felt extremely embarrassed to feel like I was "starting all over again" at the age of 30-something. I was going to be starting at the same point a five-year-old starts. But the truth is, the Quran is never finished, so there's no such thing as starting again. No matter how much we study and read and understand, the Quran will always have more to teach us. That is one of its miracles.

So I bit the bullet and started Quran classes with the same teacher who was teaching my children. I started from the very beginning: the Arabic alphabet. My teacher wanted to make sure I was pronouncing each letter correctly, and he was extremely patient and kind in the process. My anxiety and embarrassment eased immediately, and because of my classes, I read the Quran at least 5 times a week for 30 minutes. And the truth is, I loved it! As my pronunciation and speed improved, I felt more confident and thoroughly enjoyed reciting the Quran. So I encourage you as well, whether it's the first time or the fiftieth, pick up that Quran and get yourself a Quran teacher. You will never regret learning and loving the word of your Lord. You will only regret not doing it.

Exercise: Quran Activity

Grab your Quran (or use one online if you don't own one) and flip through. Stop at a random page, then a random line, and read the translation. Write how it applies to your current situation or what you can learn from it in the space you are in now. The Quran is limitless, spaceless, timeless. This is your sign to find out what Allah (swt) wants you to know.

_____

_____

_____

_____

Nubuwwah: Belief in the Prophets

Prophets and messengers are one of Allah's (swt) many mercies upon us. Earlier in this book, I talked about the original testimony: before we were born, we testified that Allah (swt) is our Lord and then we were sent to this world to worship Him. But without our fitrah and our prophets, it would be very difficult to obey Allah (swt) because even now, we get lost in the treasures and distractions of this world. So Allah (swt) gave us guides to remind us whom to worship and how to worship. Allah (swt) did not leave us stranded. He gave us the tools we need to pass the test we call *dunya*. The prophets and messengers are sent to us for that very reason.

God sends revelations through Angel Jibreel to the prophets, who pass on the message to all people and guide them. And while we should definitely love and honor our prophets, we should also remember that they are simply human just like us and not to be worshiped. They are not partners with Allah (swt) or related to Him. They are also not perfect. They are people who were chosen to share the message of tawhid.

Two Sides to Every Coin

إِنَّا أَرْسَلْنَٰكَ بِٱلْحَقِّ بَشِيرًا وَنَذِيرًا ۚ وَإِن مِّن أُمَّةٍ إِلَّا خَلَا فِيهَا نَذِيرٌ ٢٤

"We have surely sent you with the truth as a deliverer of good news and a warner. There is no community that has not had a warner." (Quran 35:24)

In the Quran, Allah (swt) also tells us that while the messengers are certainly guides and bearers of good news, they are also warners because the message tells us what happens to those who don't believe. One thing you realize about our deen is that it is indeed "the middle path." It is never healthy to be extremely on one side or another in any situation. So while we should certainly see our prophets as bearers of good news and guidance, we also have to understand that there should be a certain amount of fear as well if we don't obey. There are two sides to every coin.

Growing up, in Islamic classes I was always taught about a healthy amount of fear and hope by having it compared to the wings of a bird. One wing is hope and the other is fear, and both wings need to be steady for the bird to fly. This always made so much sense to me, and so I teach you the same thing because too much of any one thing can set an imbalance in your life. If we want to work on being strong righteous Muslims, we must practice the art of the middle path, which is exactly what all of our prophets taught us, especially the prophet of our time: Prophet Muhammad (pbuh).

I believe it's important for me to have more hope and positive reinforcement than fear and negative reinforcement so I can have a positive outlook on life and about my Lord. Of course it's always important to have a healthy amount of fear as well—and that may look different for different people. Some people are more motivated by a good outcome, and that keeps them going toward their goal while others stay on a path because they fear what will happen if they don't.

Exercise: Wings of a Bird

Use the wings below to list hopes and fears about an important aspect of your life; it can be about going to school, your job, your relationship, etc. (if you don't go to school, you'll never get a job vs. when you go to school you get to see your friends). See if you end up having more hopes or more fears to recognize if you are motivated by positive or negative reinforcement.

There are 25 prophets mentioned in the Quran and of course, our Prophet Muhammad is the best of them all. How lucky we are to be part of the *ummah*, the people, of Prophet Muhammad (pbuh).

Here are the 25 prophets of the Quran:

1. Adam (as)
2. Idris (as) (Enoch)
3. Nuh (as) (Noah)
4. Hud (as)
5. Saleh (as) (Shaleh)
6. Ibrahim (as) (Abraham)
7. Lut (as) (Lot)
8. Ismail (as) (Ishmael)
9. Ishaq (as) (Isaac)
10. Yaqub (as) (Jacob)
11. Yusuf (as) (Joseph)
12. Ayyub (as) (Job)
13. Shu'aib (as) (Jethro)
14. Musa (as) (Moses)
15. Harun (as) (Aaron)
16. Dzulkifli (as) (Ezekiel)
17. Dawud (as) (David)
18. Sulaiman (as) (Solomon)
19. Ilyas (as) (Elijah)
20. Alyas'a (as) (Elisha)
21. Yunus (as) (Jonah)
22. Zakaria (as) (Zachariah)
23. Yahya (as) (John)
24. Isa (as) (Jesus)
25. Muhammad (pbuh)

Akhirah: Belief in the Day of Judgment and the Afterlife

The Quran breaks up our lives into two parts:

The dunya: the temporary worldly life we live in now.

The akhirah: the afterlife, which is infinite and starts after our death in the dunya.

The akhirah is a part of ghayb, the unseen, because anyone who has seen it cannot come back and tell us about it, and once we are in it, it will be too late to come back and change the way we lived in this world. What we know about the akhirah is what Allah (swt) has taught us in His revelations and what the Prophet (pbuh) has told us about it. But we know for sure that the akhirah is real. We are on this earth simply to reach the akhirah one day because we know that this world is a test and not the ultimate resting place.

CHARACTERISTICS OF DUNYA	CHARACTERISTICS OF AKHIRAH
⁕ Temporary	⁕ Permanent
⁕ Starts before death	⁕ Starts after worldly death
⁕ A test: spheres of actions	⁕ Spheres of results
⁕ Fleeting	⁕ Infinite
⁕ Distraction	⁕ True pleasure or pain
⁕ Less important	⁕ More important
⁕ Illusion	

٦٤ َنوُمَلْعَي اوُناَك ْوَل ۚ ُناَوَيَحْلا َيِهَل َةَرِخآْلا َراَّدلا َّنِإَو ۚ ٌبِعَلَو ٌوْهَل اَّلِإ اَيْنُّدلا ُةاَيَحْلا ِهِذَٰه اَمَو

"This worldly life is no more than play and amusement. But the Hereafter is indeed the real life, if only they knew." (Quran 29:64)

If we could realize the true temporary nature of the dunya, we would truly live this life the way it is supposed to be lived: like a test. When we watch a TV show or a sports event, even if it's two hours long, whether we go watch it in person or on a screen, we know that that event is just entertainment. It is not our real lives and in general we do not change our whole lives, our livelihood, our families, our jobs, or our responsibilities for two hours of entertainment. So why is it that we are willing to sacrifice our entire akhirah, an infinite life, for something so short lived?

Because we forget. We get lost. We confuse this life for the next one. We start thinking we are never going to die, even when Allah (swt) sends us signs to remind us, even when people we love die around us. We are blinded by the shimmer of this world, and honestly, that's the biggest misfortune of all.

١١٢ َنيِنِس َدَدَع ِضْرَأْلا يِف ْمُتْثِبَل ْمَك َلاَق

١١٣ َنيِّداَعْلا ِلَأْساَف ٍمْوَي َضْعَب ْوَأ اًمْوَي اَنْثِبَل اوُلاَق

"He will ask them, 'How many years did you remain on earth?' They will reply, 'We remained only a day or part of a day.' But ask those who kept count." (Quran 23:112–113)

Allah (swt) tells us how we will remember this world, even if we live to be 100: it will feel like we were only on this Earth for a day or so. Think about your life up until now. Whether you are 17 years old or 56. Look back on your years. For me, that's 35 years of memories, of life, but how much do I really even remember? If I sat and tried to remember everything I did and go through my life, it wouldn't take too long because the truth is I don't remember much. It all becomes a blur, a dream of which you remember only vague parts. And on the Day of Judgment when we meet our Lord, will this life be worth it?

Will the few memories and vague moments of pleasure be worth an eternity of damnation?

In the Quran, Allah (swt) calls himself:

مَـٰلِكِ يَوْمِ ٱلدِّينِ ٤

"Master of the Day of Judgment." (Quran 1:4)

Allah (swt) is the only one who can judge our actions and decide our ultimate resting place: *jannah* or *jahannum*, heaven or hell. Our job is our efforts in this world. How hard and how often are we trying to obey the commands of Allah (swt)? How often do we remember Allah (swt)? How often do we do the things that Allah (swt) told us and avoid the things we have been told to avoid?

Here's the fact of life: we are not perfect. We have free will. And we will make mistakes. Allah (swt) knows this. But that's why a lot of being Muslim is about our intention. Do we intend to do good and put in effort for that good? The results, the victories, the losses—those are not in our hands; just our efforts are in our control. And being a Muslim isn't just about the dos and don'ts; it's about your character as well.

Muslims have beautiful characters, at least, we're supposed to. So as you continue to work on your iman, your faith, and work to incorporate the pillars and commands of Allah (swt) into your life, remember that good character, morals, ethics, and manners are fundamental to our deen and the means by which we can truly gain salvation in the life to come.

I've run into so many people in my life who pray five times a day, don't miss a single fast, dress in accordance with Islamic laws, and outwardly seem like the most pious Muslims, but they are arrogant, rude, and downright mean. This is not what Islam teaches us because the believers who are most beloved by Allah (swt) and His Messenger and who have the most complete faith are those with the best character.

And the most important thing to remember is that none of us, even the best of us, can ever enter jannah, paradise, without the mercy of Allah (swt). We will not get into paradise on merit alone, it is indeed Allah's (swt) mercy upon us that will allow us to enter the gardens. So while we always try our best, it's important not to become arrogant and think we've done enough good to *deserve* heaven. Sometimes, just one of your good deeds could be enough to bless you with Allah's (swt) mercy.

I pray we are all blessed with Allah's (swt) mercy in the dunya and the akhirah. Ameen!

Exercise: A Day in Jannah

Manifestation: Imagine you are in your akhirah. Allah (swt) has blessed you with His infinite mercy and allowed you to enter Jannat-al-Firdous, the highest level of paradise. You step into your ultimate resting place, where everything is perfect. Everything you ever wanted is within reach and everyone you ever loved is with you. What do you see? What can you do? Who are you with? Write down how your first day in jannah would go and what pleasures Allah (swt) has bestowed upon you. Inshallah one day you will get all of it and more.

THE NEW MUSLIM WORKBOOK

Al Qadr: Belief in Predestination

Qadr can be defined as predestination, or destiny, and it's the understanding that everything that happens is decreed by God and known by God. Allah (swt) knows the past, present, and future, and nothing can happen without His will.

Qadr is a belief that can be difficult to make sense of as human beings because our knowledge is so limited. People have a hard time rectifying exactly how qadr is possible or what it means because they tend to confuse how free will and qadr can exist simultaneously.

"If everything is decreed by Allah, do we even have free will?"

That's often the logic I've heard, and the truth is, we don't have all the answers. I'm sure scholars could explain it better than I can but there are two ways I rectify what I understand about destiny and free will. To me, the two are not contradictory at all. We *do* have free will, Allah (swt) said so. But everything is decreed by Allah (swt) because he allows us to make those decisions. And since He is not limited to time the way we are, He knows the past, the present, and the future, so he knows what choices we will make and what actions we will take even before we take them. Allah (swt) is not limited to the physical laws of this world the way we are, and He is capable of so much more. This fact alone leaves me in awe of my Creator; he is boundless in every way while we are so limited.

In the Quran, Allah (swt) explains:

وَكَذَٰلِكَ جَعَلْنَا لِكُلِّ نَبِىٍّ عَدُوًّا شَيَٰطِينَ ٱلْإِنسِ وَٱلْجِنِّ يُوحِى بَعْضُهُمْ إِلَىٰ بَعْضٍ زُخْرُفَ ٱلْقَوْلِ غُرُورًا ۚ وَلَوْ شَآءَ رَبُّكَ مَا فَعَلُوهُ ۖ فَذَرْهُمْ وَمَا يَفْتَرُونَ ١١٢

"And so We have made for every prophet enemies—devilish humans and jinn—whispering to one another with elegant words of deception. Had it been your Lord's Will, they would not have done such a thing. So leave them and their deceit." (Quran 6:112)

Belief in qadr is something that gives me so much solace because nothing in this world can happen without Allah (swt), even something seemingly "bad." Evil cannot reach us if Allah (swt) does not will it to and if it does, then there must be some good in it. It was allowed for a reason and knowing that Allah (swt) is *Ar-Rahman Ar-Raheem*, that Most Merciful and the Most Gracious, only good can come of it as long as we get closer to Allah (swt) and increase our connection and faith in Him.

So when things get tough or you start to fear people who want to harm you or talk badly about you, remember that nothing in this world happens without Allah's (swt) decree. If something happened to you, it was meant for you. Our job is to consistently pray for Allah's (swt) mercy in all that happens to us and to get closer to Him.

If we do, we have nothing to worry about.

Chapter Summary Exercise: Never Stop Learning

What is something new I learned from this chapter, either about Islam or myself?

_____

_____

_____

_____

_____

_____

What am I grateful for today?

_____

_____

_____

_____

_____

_____

How did I lean on Allah (swt) today?

_____

_____

_____

_____

_____

_____

Is there anyone I can forgive today? Or is there someone I should reach out to for forgiveness?

_____

_____

_____

_____

_____

_____

Chapter 5

HARAM AND HALAL: IT'S THE DOS AND DON'TS

Many years ago when I was working as a radiation therapist, I was wearing my *hijab*, my headscarf. Now even though it was 2015 at the time and I lived near a heavily Muslim and Arab populated area in Dearborn, Michigan, some of my coworkers (who were perfectly lovely and kind) knew nothing about Muslims and had never met one. Really, in this day and age where it seems like Muslims are at every corner, where Muslims are becoming elected officials, where Muslims are just as much part of this society as everyone else, they knew nothing more than what they'd seen in the news.

And we all know very well how Muslims are portrayed in the news.

I could tell that my coworkers, we'll call them Stacie and Tina, were a little uncomfortable around me, especially because I was wearing a hijab. It's like when you walk into a room and people get quiet or stop making jokes and you just know it's because you're there so you just kind of wish the ground would open up and swallow you whole to avoid the awkwardness.

But knowing full well that the ground wasn't going to open up and free me from my predicament, I decided to make the people around me comfortable the best way I knew how. I put a big smile on my face and joked about them feeling weird around me.

"Honestly guys, I'm pretty normal! You can ask me anything you want if you have any questions."

And boy did they have questions!

Are you allowed to shave your legs?

Can you really not eat pork?

Do you wear your headscarf at home?

Are you allowed to date?

So then how did you meet your husband?

Honestly, their questions were so simple that it shocked me how little they knew. Stacie actually told me that she lives in an area that is basically all white. She hadn't even seen a person of color until she was about 11 years old and her family went to Disney World. I was shocked that there were people like that in the world. But there are! Not everyone is living in an urban center where people mix and mingle with people of other cultures and races.

The great thing was that after that day, Stacie and Tina were so relaxed around me. I was just one of the girls, no longer defined by my hijab. The next day, Stacie told a coworker who wasn't there the day before, "You can talk about whatever. She's totally normal!"

I kid you not, that seriously happened. And to be quite honest it kind of shocked me. Their questions weren't about terrorism or what I think about bombs. They weren't crazy, deep questions that questioned my morality and humanity. They were just simple questions about everyday issues. They really just wanted to know the dos and don'ts because sometimes it seems like we have a lot of them.

But the truth is we can do a lot more as Muslims than we cannot. We have a lot more *halal*, permissible or permitted, than we have *haram*, impermissible or forbidden. But for some reason, people seem to get really hung up on the haram instead. In general however, the default is that everything is halal unless it has been stated to be haram.

Exercise: Can vs. Can't

How do you view the dos and don'ts of Islam? Do you feel like Islam has "too many rules?" List all the things you can do and the things you cannot. Do you think you need to shift your mindset to focus on the halal instead of the haram?

Allah (swt), our Lord, is the only one who can tell us what is haram and what is halal. One thing we tend to find in our community is a lot of people using the word "haram" to shame people. They see something they don't like and it's often a shake of the head and a condescending "Haram!" in your direction. This isn't to say we shouldn't try to guide one another when we see wrong being done, but unfortunately shaming many times seems to be the goal.

Even within our deen, there are differences of opinion on many concepts. This is an area of *fiqh*, deep understanding of Islamic laws that I wouldn't dare get into, but some of the most obvious and undisputed haram is:

* Drinking
* Gambling
* Murder
* Giving or receiving interest, as with loans
* Wearing silk or gold (men)
* Eating pork
* Eating from an animal that was already found dead
* Magic
* Adultery (or acts that lead to adultery)
* Arrogance
* Lying
* Cheating

What are some impermissible actions that you did before that you now have to stop as you get closer to Allah (swt)? What are some commanded or encouraged actions that you want to start? What are behaviors/actions that don't need to change? What are actions you anticipate might be difficult to change? How do you plan on overcoming these challenges?

ACTIONS TO STOP	ACTIONS TO START	CHALLENGES

Allah (swt) is extremely merciful in all His decisions for us. Whether we are doing something positive or avoiding a negative, it's best to remember that Allah (swt) has commanded this for a reason that is beneficial to us, whether we understand it or not. And there were times when things were permissible but were made forbidden later on.

Muslims used to be allowed to drink alcohol during the Prophet's (pbuh) time. The Arabs of that time were actually heavy drinkers, but slowly, it was made forbidden. However, Allah (swt) didn't just say, "Thou shall stop drinking immediately!" and then suddenly everyone stopped. That wouldn't have been possible obviously because of the addictive nature of alcohol.

First, we were told not to drink while praying. Then we were told of its negative effects to help us understand why it was being prohibited, and eventually we were told to stop drinking it at all because of its addictive nature, the harm it causes to the body, and how it clouds one's judgment.

I think as Muslims we tend to get lost in the dos and don'ts, the allowed and the not allowed. And don't get me wrong, we absolutely should be obeying Allah's (swt) commands for the sole reason that our Lord commanded it. But I want us to remember: we're human beings, not angels. We have desires. We have free will. We have needs and wants, and sometimes we are selfish. We will sin, whether we like it or not.

But that doesn't mean we stop being a Muslim. It doesn't mean we give up or lose hope. It means we continue to work on ourselves every day and seek closeness with God. It means, when we sin, we repent immediately. We absolutely know that Allah's (swt) mercy is immense and that no sin stands in comparison to Allah's (swt) forgiveness.

The Devil Whispers

The *shaytan*, the devil, has a sneaky way of making us feel so ashamed that we think we are not worthy of seeking forgiveness, especially right after a sin. But his trick is to make us think Allah (swt) will not forgive us. His trick is to make us hopeless in Allah's (swt) mercy.

How can Allah (swt) forgive me after what I've just done?

I don't deserve Allah's (swt) mercy.

I've already sinned so much, might as well keep going.

I haven't prayed in three months, what's the point in starting now?

This type of negative talk is the whisper of shaytan to have us doubt Allah (swt). But no matter how much haram you've committed in your past and no matter how many commands you've neglected, it is never too late to seek Allah's (swt) mercy as long as you are breathing. Allah's (swt) mercy and forgiveness is much bigger than anything else, and Allah (swt) tells us if we seek forgiveness, He will forgive us as long as we are sincere.

In the Quran, Allah (swt) reminds us of His mercy:

١١٠ اٖمِيحَّر اٗروُفَغَ ةَللآ ِدجَي ةَللآ ِرفْغَتْسَي مَُّث ُهَسفْنَ مِلْظَي وْأَ اءَوُس ْلَمْعَي نَمَو

"And whoever does a wrong or wrongs himself but then seeks forgiveness of Allah will find Allah Forgiving and Merciful.'" (Quran 4:110)

Conditions of Repentance

How do we seek forgiveness?

As I mentioned before, we do not need an intercessor to connect to our Lord. We do not need a confessional, and we do not need to go to a mosque to repent. The beauty and ease of our deen is that we can seek *istagfaar*, repentance, anywhere and anytime.

There are some conditions when we do seek Allah's (swt) forgiveness:

1. Stop the sin.

2. Feel regret or remorse over committing the sin

3. Make a conscious intention to give up the sin.

4. Restore people's rights/property if the sin involved wronging someone else.

Now. what if you make an intention to never commit the sin again, but then you make the same mistake?

Repent again! Keep repenting until one day you never return to the sin. But always seek the mercy of the Most Merciful. The dos and don'ts aren't there to box us in or scare us. They are there to protect us in this worldly life, for our benefit and to keep us close to Allah (swt) and always remember Him.

Chapter Summary Exercise: Never Stop Learning

Write a letter to your Lord. Tell Allah (swt) about a sin you might be struggling with and something you want to change for the better in your life. Ask him for forgiveness and guidance on how you can change.

_____

_____

_____

_____

_____

What is something new I learned from this chapter, either about Islam or myself?

_____

_____

_____

_____

_____

What am I grateful for today?

_____

_____

_____

_____

_____

How did I lean on Allah (swt) today?

_____

_____

_____

_____

_____

Is there anyone I can forgive today? Or is there someone I should reach out to for forgiveness?

_____

_____

_____

_____

_____

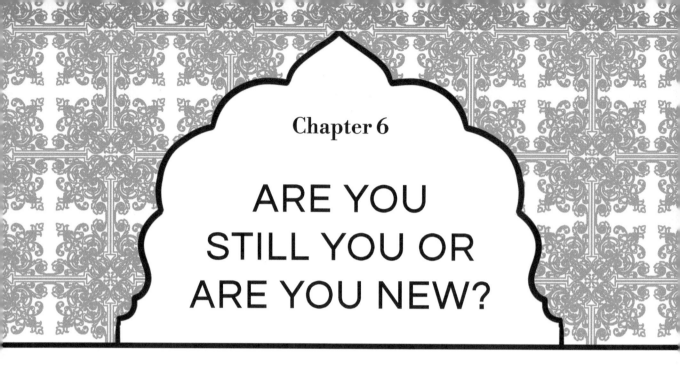

Chapter 6

ARE YOU STILL YOU OR ARE YOU NEW?

Whether you are a revert or a Muslim who is finding Allah (swt) again, there are challenges you will face along the way. (Muslims prefer to use the term "revert" instead of "convert" since we believe all people are born believing in Allah [swt].) One of the major challenges is your own identity.

Who are you?

Who are you outside of being a Muslim?

How does your previous life and identity fit into this new life you are trying to build?

How do you center God in your life without losing who you are as a person?

I imagine all of us as our own solar systems. For a while, we've been orbiting other things or people, maybe even ourselves. But every time we reconnect with Allah (swt), we shift our entire system to orbit Him instead. Every planet, every moon, everything has to shift to revolve around our new source of light: God. But that shift is not an easy one to make. Some planets might not change course as fast as they need to while others may change too quickly. It takes time for everything to fall into place.

So the question is, is this a new solar system altogether? Or is it the same?

Think about your personal solar system. Now that you are on this journey of shifting your solar system to orbit Allah (swt), what will lose its place? What will become more important. What things will leave the solar system completely or lose significance, and how long do you think it'll take for you to get comfortable in your new system?

_____

_____

_____

_____

Most of the reverts I've talked to face the struggle of an identity crisis because there is so much change in their life once they find Islam and it's hard to decipher what parts of yourself stay the same, what changes, and who you are now. So let's talk about some of the practical challenges you might face in this new chapter of your life and how you can best prepare to overcome them.

Religion or Culture

The first issue often arises because the religion and its practices are often tied to cultural practices of many born Muslims. This can be hard to differentiate and cause confusion. Many of my friends who reverted to Islam were often heavily influenced and highly motivated by a group of friends. Because of the connection to their group who tended to be from the same region, my revert friends would take on the cultural practices of the born Muslim as well. While that's completely understandable and allowed, what happens is that reverts may lose their own cultural identity down the line. While they can adopt and enjoy someone else's cultural practices, they will likely still feel excluded at times, which is why holding on to your own identity is vital.

This doesn't just happen with reverts either. It can happen with born Muslims who find the religion again. When I was younger, my group of friends were almost exclusively Arab so when we started practicing more, I gave up some of my Pakistani culture and adopted their Arab practices. Of course, there is nothing wrong with that, but it did make me feel out of touch sometimes. Eventually however, I grew up and became more confident in being able to enjoy my own culture while still following Islamic practices. But this journey takes time, sometimes months and sometimes years.

As a revert, it's important to keep hold of your own culture and traditions as well. The beautiful thing about our deen is that it is inclusive. It is not limited to only one culture, country, or language. Islam is often confused with the culture of Arabs but the two are not the same. There are many Arabs who are Christians, Jews, and even atheists. And of course, there are many Muslims who are not Arab. Islam is not exclusive and does not favor anyone based on their nationality, skin color, gender, age, or anything else. The only thing that makes one Muslim better than another is their iman and their heart, and that can only be judged by Allah (swt).

While it's great to enjoy other cultures, foods, clothes, and traditions, just remember to cherish yours as well so you don't feel lost down the line.

Exercise: Old and New You

What is your identity/culture vs. the identity/culture of those who influenced your faith? How can you balance enjoying a new culture while holding on to your own?

THE NEW MUSLIM WORKBOOK

My Family, Your Family

Family is one of the most important things to me in life, after my religion, of course. Allah (swt) blessed us with our family for a reason. He picked people for us that we can never break ties with because no matter what, your relatives and family will always be connected by blood. Even if you fight, even if you never talk again, your father will always be your father and your mother will always be your mother. However, many reverts go through a really difficult time with their families when they decide to become a Muslim because leaving the religion they were brought up with in the home can feel like breaking ties with the core value system of the family itself.

Ironically, even some Muslim parents and families may have issues if you start becoming "too religious." Muslims who find the deen again can sometimes face ridicule and be judged as to why they are turning into a *molvi* (a Muslim scholar or Quran teacher but the term can sometimes be used in a derogatory way to make someone seem too extreme) or if they think they're better than the rest of the family.

Changing your entire belief system or changing the way you practice it can be devastating to your family because, at its core, it's a hit to the ego. It's the very essence of questioning someone's faith when you leave it, even if you are not asking them to leave it. It's saying, "You were doing it wrong, and I am going to do it right."

It's not uncommon for reverts to be disowned and lose all support—physical, mental, spiritual, and financial—when they become Muslims. Reverts whose families and friends aren't Muslim are often in very vulnerable positions, and I believe this is often their first test from Allah (swt). Make sure you have a support system in place if possible. Not only will they be the ones you reach out to for help and guidance on how to do things, but they can also support you emotionally.

As born Muslims with strong support systems, a lifelong community, and Muslim families, it's our job to offer support and help in any way we can. But if you find yourself in this position, make sure you are reaching out and staying in touch with friends and community members who can guide you.

Holidays like Eid and Ramadan when people spend time with their families can be lonely for reverts because their families aren't Muslim and don't celebrate the same way. You may feel isolated, alone, or just plain bored. It may not feel like a holiday if you don't have family to celebrate with, so it's important to plan ahead. Be proactive in planning with others, and reach out to friends whom you could spend time with, especially if you can join in with other families to avoid feeling the loneliness that can come with being a revert.

The start of something new is beautiful, especially when it's the start of a relationship with Allah (swt), but it also means that something else has ended. It's okay to mourn the end of certain things in your life, while looking forward to the blessings that are coming your way, and to prepare for the changes.

Exercise: Friends Who Are Family

There are times you will need a friend to turn to in this journey of life. Allah (swt) has given us relationships to fulfill certain needs. Think about the people in your life who you can turn to for each situation. It can be the same person or multiple people.

A friend that is like family: _____

A friend I can turn to when I'm feeling lonely: _____

A friend I can turn to when I need religious uplifting and guidance: _____

A friend I can turn to when I want to have fun: _____

A friend I can spend Eid or a holiday with: _____

A friend who I can go to the mosque with: _____

A friend that is positive and helps me feel grateful: _____

A friend who can listen: _____

Who Are You?

I see myself as a Muslim, a woman, a mom, a wife, a daughter, a sister, a Pakistani, an American, a Canadian, a friend, an aunt, a writer, a content creator, and many other labels. But I think that there are many other people in the world who can have the exact same labels as me. So how am I different from them? And if I change one of those labels, do I stop being myself?

What makes me a unique person? What makes me who I am?

I think we associate ourselves to our labels so much that we think we *are* our labels. But we are more than our labels; we are a compilation of what we are, what we believe, how we think, our memories, our attributes, our characteristics, our personality, and the type of person we are. And when we find a new system of belief or renew our intention within that belief system, we may feel lost or confused because we think we have to be a brand-new person and figure it out all over again. This type of identity crisis can be detrimental to a person because you begin to question the essence of who you are.

But you are still you!

Remember, you are the same solar system, even if what you're orbiting has changed.

Your Creator, the Fashioner, the Source of Love made you exactly as you are for a reason. He did not make a mistake that requires you to become someone else or someone new. Allah (swt) does everything in His most infinite knowledge and wisdom, and you were created to be the person you are, to get to this point in your life, and to find Him, love Him, worship Him, and be connected to Him.

Exercise: You Are YOU

What type of person are you? What are your characteristics and personality traits? List your traits, your labels, your characteristics, the parts of you that you love and that make you, you! Look back on these often to remind yourself who you are, and remember: you don't have to change them even as you get closer to God.

WHAT MAKES ME, ME

1.	
2.	
3.	
4.	
5.	
6.	
7.	
8.	
9.	
10.	

Do not feel pressured to change the type of person you are in order to worship Allah (swt) because the two are not mutually exclusive. The confusion and pressure come when we think our personality clashes with the morals of Islam. For example, because *haaya*, modesty, and humility are valued and taught in our deen, people who are extroverted and outgoing may face an identity crisis. Haaya is confused with being quiet and timid, and often women especially are pressured into changing their personality to become a better Muslim.

But there is nothing wrong with being extroverted and outgoing if that's the type of person you are. It's wonderful to be exactly how Allah (swt) created you, and following the commands of Allah (swt) and practicing haaya doesn't mean you become quiet. It means you can dress more modestly and be aware of how you interact with the opposite gender by not spending time alone with them or touching them, but it doesn't mean you can't be friendly.

It's also about replacing haram with halal. If as an extrovert you go out many nights to bars and clubs with your friends and hang out, replace the impermissible social event with a permissible social event instead. Plan weekly girls' nights or join a sports team. It's a balance of being yourself and following Allah's (swt) commands, which is possible. It's just a matter of being more mindful.

But going against the type of person Allah (swt) made you will have you feeling like you lost yourself. Allah (swt) made you as you are, and He guided you to Him. That means both things can coexist beautifully.

Exercise: The Replacements

Think about the type of person you are and what you like to do. Is there any haram in your life that needs to be replaced? What haram can be replaced with halal that still allow you to feel fulfilled in a similar manner?

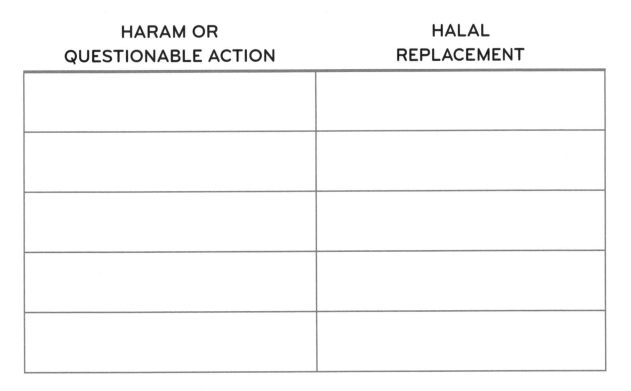

HARAM OR QUESTIONABLE ACTION	HALAL REPLACEMENT

Frenemies

A lot of who we think we are has to do with who we spend the most time with: our friends and family. We already talked about problems that may arise in your family setting as you take a journey to connect with Allah (swt), because not everyone is on that journey with you, and it can naturally create distance, but there are also friends in our life that play a big role in who we are and how we act.

"We are the average of the five people we spend the most time with."

Jim Rohn's famous quote is based on the law of averages. Whether we like it or not, whether we believe it or not, we are heavily influenced by our friends and those we spend the most time with. This concept was even shared by our Prophet (pbuh).

According to a hadith of the Prophet (pbuh), "Man is influenced by the faith of his friends. Therefore, be careful of whom you befriend."

Since we are social creatures who crave and desire social interactions, love, and bonding with others, it is important that our friends and those closest to us remind us of our Lord. But when we get closer to Allah (swt), especially as a revert, it is likely that those we were spending time with weren't reminding us of our Lord, or maybe we were engaging in social activities that were not compatible with Islamic values. Losing such "friends" is actually a blessing because those who take you away from your Lord are not friends; they are enemies, and it could be that those very people could be the reason you end up being punished in the akhirah.

Even though it may be good for you to lose certain people in your life, you still may feel like you lost a part of yourself. Losing your closest social circle can be devastating to your identity, especially if you spend a lot of time with them. Mentally, it is better to be prepared to lose those who were close to you as you make this transition. If you don't lose your friends, then you will appreciate them even more for supporting you, and if you do lose them, you will accept it more easily and quickly.

But remember, your Lord is your biggest and best friend and companion, and He will replace what has been lost with something and someone even better. Your Lord knows who is best for you on this journey. He knows who will help you and support you, and He also knows who will bring you down, so if Allah (swt) does make space in your life, just trust and have tawakkul that He is bringing you an ever bigger gift. Our Lord will never leave us and maybe He is emptying our hearts so that we can fill it with Him before he brings us people and blessings we can hold in our hands.

May Allah (swt) always give us good companions, friends, and mentors who remind us of our Lord and bring us closer to Allah (swt).

Ameen!

Chapter Summary Exercise: Never Stop Learning

Have you ever lost a friend or someone in your life you didn't imagine? Think back to that time. Who was it? How prominent was that person in your life? How did you part ways, and how did you accept that loss? What blessings came into your life since then?

_____

_____

_____

_____

_____

What is something new I learned from this chapter, either about Islam or myself?

_____

_____

_____

_____

What am I grateful for today?

_____

_____

_____

_____

_____

How did I lean on Allah (swt) today?

_____

_____

_____

_____

_____

Is there anyone I can forgive today? Or is there someone I should reach out to for forgiveness?

_____

_____

_____

_____

_____

Chapter 7

HATERS GONNA HATE: ISLAMOPHOBIA

Look, I'm just going to get right into it and address the elephant in the room, or should I say, the book: you're probably going to be called a terrorist at some point, or maybe you already have.

Being a practicing Muslim, getting close to Allah (swt), and loving your deen means you might be questioned about believing in a "radical" religion, especially if you live in a Western country.

Islamophobia is real. Sometimes it is blatant and in your face, but more often than not, it is quiet, something that lingers silently under the surface. It is often so subtle that you can barely just feel it, but if you call someone out, they can gaslight you into thinking you're being sensitive and overthinking. It can be the raise of an eyebrow or a small smirk that leaves a bad taste in your mouth. The fact is that for many years, the world has thrown out this image of us wearing long black capes with bombs strapped to our chests, or being uneducated and backward, and that type of rhetoric isn't forgotten easily. And it'll leave you with the urge to defend your humanity and defend your choices.

Have you ever faced Islamophobia? Or has anyone ever questioned your decision to practice your faith? Write about a time when you felt pressured or attacked for either being a Muslim or being interested in Islam. How did you deal with it? Did it make you question yourself? Did your confidence falter? If so, what can you do to help overcome those pressures?

_____

_____

_____

_____

_____

_____

The American Dream

I wish I didn't have to convince people of my humanity. I wish I could continue to live my mediocre life without all the extra "proving myself" and public "condemning." Actually, I'm going to correct myself (yes, yes, I can be wrong sometimes, too. Shocking, I know!); we don't want to live mediocre lives. We want to live amazing and fulfilling lives. As Muslims, we really strive to be great. As a matter of fact, we don't really even have a choice in the matter.

As a Muslim who lives in a Western country, I grew up with strict parents who taught me and my siblings that we *have* to be great. We grew up knowing that our parents or grandparents gave up a life in their own country so that they could give their children a life of more opportunities: the American dream. And it may sound amazing and motivational, but really it's just emotional blackmail that we face our entire lives. Not to mention the fact that the American dream turned out more like a nightmare, with us facing Islamophobia on one side and an identity crisis on the other.

Ahhh, the American dream indeed.

I, like many other Muslims, grew up being told that I *had* to be a doctor. Seriously, that was the only choice given. I didn't even know there were other jobs in the world that mattered. The fact that I didn't become one is an atrocity and a miracle all at once. But the truth is we are ambitious, smart, and kind, so it feels pretty horrible when people who aren't Muslims and don't know anything about Muslims want to portray us as bigots who love bombs and hate the West. It's exhausting being guilty at first sight, and that is something you might have to face from time to time.

There are many things that are used against us, but there is one concept that is used to justify Islamophobia the most: *jihad*.

Most people think it means "holy war" but that is just the skewed, tainted version of a beautiful word. Jihad literally means "struggle."

There can be many types of jihad because obviously there can be many types of struggles. Yes, you can struggle in war, but what it often refers to is an internal struggle within the self by controlling your desires and following the commands of God. Because let's be honest, it's not always easy following the commands and laws of any religion. Life itself is one big jihad because it is a test, after all.

┌─────────────────────────────────────┐
Exercise: Life Is a Battlefield
└─────────────────────────────────────┘

What is your jihad? Is there an aspect of Islam that you are struggling to incorporate in your life? Is there a command you are struggling to follow? Is there a haram you are struggling to stop? Why is it difficult, and what is your plan of action to overcome this jihad?

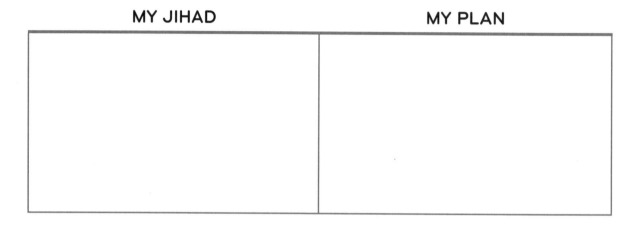

MY JIHAD	MY PLAN

Guilty Until Proven Innocent

As someone who is an active Muslim, I recognize there is a burden that is placed on our shoulders to prove our humanity, to condemn any violence by someone who claims to be Muslim, because the assumption is that we naturally don't. You likely won't have the luxury of being innocent until proven guilty anymore.

I think that's why more people of color and minorities are woke. We don't have the luxury of saying, "I don't like to get political." Our color, our race, our beliefs, our whole damn life is political. We can't sleep through politics. We can't sleep through the news. We can't sleep through the violence. We have to be constantly aware and ready to defend ourselves.

The trouble with being woke is that you can never really sleep again.

Let me tell you what happens when a "Muslim" or an Arab or a brown-skinned person does something bad: we all get the blame. And I say "Muslim" because many times when there is a terror attack, the person claiming to be a Muslim is doing what is inherently against Islam. We all have to defend ourselves. We all have to openly state that we condemn this act of violence because the assumption is that we agree with it or sympathize with it. Anytime something comes up in the news about an attack or a shooter, Muslims sit there watching the news and holding our breaths. We feel pain for the victims and watch intently as the story unfolds and we think to ourselves,

"Please don't let it be a Muslim. Please, God, don't let it be a Muslim."

I *hate* that feeling. It's a feeling of complete hopelessness and hopefulness at the same time. It's a feeling of jumping out of an airplane and leaving your stomach behind, just waiting and hoping it'll come back into place. It's a feeling of guilt, because we let out a sigh of relief when the shooter ends up being white or some sort of non-Muslim, even though innocent lives have been lost. But more likely than not, if the story is big enough, then, sure enough, a little while later, he does end up associating himself with Islam and all you see across the screen is "Radical Islamic Terrorism."

I remember when the San Bernardino attack happened. I was working at the hospital and the story was unfolding while we were treating patients. And of course, everyone was keeping an eye on what was happening. As a radiation therapist, you treat a patient every 15 minutes, so every time a patient would come in, they would talk about the story and show concern, and I swear to God, I was sweating bullets the entire time.

There I was, a visible Muslim woman, treating patients and being my usual amazing, helpful self, but in the back of my mind, I kept wondering what the patients would think if this attack ended up being associated with Islam somehow.

Would they wonder about me? Would they assume I was somehow happy about the attack? That I sympathized with the attackers? Would I have to condemn the attack out loud so everyone could hear, but casual enough so that I didn't sound too defensive?

And as we kept updating the web page, I remember my coworker saying that someone saw three people in military gear. So, I secretly let out a sigh of relief, you know, assuming maybe it wasn't anything Islam-related after all. But then, of course, somehow the story turned around and it ended up being two people, a "Muslim" husband and wife duo, who even had a baby, and I remember thinking to myself:

What the hell? This doesn't even make any sense!

But there it was across the bottom of the screen: Radical Islamic Terrorism.

And before I could make sense of any of it, I was feeling guilty for something that had nothing to do with me. And my casual but concerned condemnation began.

Exercise: It Wasn't Me!

Have you ever experienced facing the backlash after an attack that was said to be Islamically motivated? Think back to that time. What happened? How did you feel? Did you feel a burden to condemn? If you weren't Muslim at the time, what did you think about Muslims after such an event?

Islamophobia isn't anything new. It isn't a twenty-first century problem, and it isn't limited to Western countries. The Prophet (pbuh) faced Islamophobia almost all his life, from the time he got his first revelation more than 1,400 years ago, even though he was always known as someone who was honest and truthful. Muslims first practiced in secret because Islam was a threat to the standard of living at the time: idol worshiping. However, nothing can be a secret forever, and when the Muslims did openly declare their faith, they were persecuted horribly for years by the Quraysh for being Muslims.

They were humiliated, attacked, and killed. Their mothers and fathers were tortured in the most brutal of ways. They were victimized and taunted. The first Muslims, including our beloved Prophet (pbuh), faced persecution for 13 years in Mecca before they migrated to Medina for safety.

So being a Muslim means that we do carry these burdens as well. While it's important to pray and partake in the ritualistic aspect of our faith, it's also necessary to live in this world and deal with what society throws our way, just as Muslims did before us.

So when you do get closer to Allah (swt), there are bound to be obstacles in the way. People will question you when you are on your journey, especially if you were once on the same path as them. Remember that the bumps on the road to Allah (swt) are Allah's (swt) blessings and tests. This isn't always an easy path to walk, so Allah (swt) strengthens us. He tests our patience, and He sends us obstacles that will remind us of Him. When Allah (swt) loves us, which He does (reading these words is proof of it), He sends us trials and tribulations so we do not forget Him. He sends us tests so we turn to Him and ask Him for guidance, and remember Him.

As long as you stay strong in your conviction to connect with Allah (swt), then Allah (swt) will reward you on your journey with closeness to Him in the dunya and ease in the akhirah.

Chapter Summary Exercise: Never Stop Learning

What is something new I learned from this chapter, either about Islam or myself?

_____

_____

_____

_____

_____

What am I grateful for today?

_____

_____

_____

_____

_____

How did I lean on Allah (swt) today?

_____

_____

_____

_____

_____

Is there anyone I can forgive today? Or is there someone I should reach out to for forgiveness?

_____

_____

_____

_____

_____

Chapter 8

FRIENDS AND FOES: COMMUNITY

One part of being a Muslim that many people underestimate but is actually a big part of who we are and how we practice is our community. The people we surround ourselves with have the ability to influence us in positive or negative ways, and our community is no different. Whether you are a new Muslim, a practicing Muslim, or a Muslim who is trying to get closer to Allah (swt), it's very important to be connected with others in your community who can lift you up when you are down, who remind you of our Lord, who encourage you to partake in Islamic activities or help others, and who help you celebrate our deen because being a Muslim all by yourself can get very lonely.

One of the best and easiest ways to become part of the Muslim community and get closer to Allah (swt) is to get involved in the local mosque. The *masjid* should truly be your point of reference because you can find like-minded people there whose goal is also to connect with and worship our Lord.

I've moved around a lot in my life and it's never easy making new friends and getting involved in a community, so my life hack has always been to go to the local mosque. I set my intention that I want to meet people and make friends who are righteous companions, who love Allah (swt) and who will remind me of my Lord. And with that intention I head to the masjid and make dua to meet good people.

And Allah (swt) has never let me down.

When I moved to downtown Chicago after I got married, it was a hard transition. I missed my family and community because I'm from a small town called Windsor, where we were all very involved in our local mosque. I didn't know how I would make friends, and we moved to the city right as Ramadan started. My husband and I went to DIC, the Downtown Islamic Center, and on the very first night we went to pray *taraweeh* salah, optional Ramadan prayers, I saw a girl who had a smile on her face and seemed so approachable. I walked up to her and asked her the time as an ice breaker, then introduced myself, mentioning that I had just moved to the city. Her name was Nadia, and she became an amazing friend to me, a blessing from Allah (swt). She invited us to an Eid dinner and introduced us to her friends, and that became our group and community in Chicago. We started a girls' *halaqa* group that met every week to discuss different Islamic topics, and we became lifelong friends.

Exercise: Community Checklist

Time to be more social and get to know your community. Take your time to complete this checklist in the hope of becoming a more active member at your mosque.

Mosque Checklist:

✳ *Introduce yourself to someone new.* [ ]

✳ *Help someone.* [ ]

✳ *Give someone a small gift, just because.* [ ]

✳ *Donate something to the mosque that someone can use (a Quran, a hijab, prayer beads, a prayer skirt, etc.) so you get a reward anytime someone uses it.* [ ]

✳ *Hold the door open for someone.* [ ]

✳ *Have a conversation with a mosque elder.* [ ]

✳ *Attend a funeral prayer for a community member.* [ ]

✳ *Volunteer at an event.* [ ]

✳ *Clean something or put something back in its proper place.* [ ]

Your iman is on a roller coaster. It will never stay in one place. Some days you will feel so connected to Allah (swt) while other times in your life you may feel at an all-time low. When you are at your lows or struggling, it is the best time to start going to the mosque more often and connecting with God and people who are connected to God.

Growing up in a small town, I always found the mosque to be a special and blessed place, and it can be for all Muslims as long as we have good intentions to get connected with Allah (swt). While the mosque is known to be a place of worship, it holds so much more value.

Exercise: Be Informed

Get to know your mosque and community.

QUESTION	ANSWER
What is the name of my local mosque?	
What is the address?	
What is the phone number?	
What is the email?	
What is my imam's (leader's) name?	
How do I contact my imam?	
What activities and classes does my mosque offer that I could take part in?	

Islam isn't an individualistic religion. If it were, I think it would actually be a lot easier in many ways. Just focus on yourself, worship Allah (swt) in your solitude, and do you. But that is not what Islam is about at all. The reason we are taught to have good character is because we have to live in this world—with all the people and things in it.

A lot of what we do and our commands are based on living within a community and how to deal with others. Zakat and sadaqah are about helping others and giving to those in need. Hajj is done with million and millions of people, not a solitary worship. We are encouraged to care about human rights, about those who are suffering and struggling, and we are taught to speak out when we see oppression.

وَاعْبُدُوا اللّٰهَ وَلَا تُشْرِكُوا بِهٖ شَيْئًا ۗ وَبِالْوَالِدَيْنِ اِحْسَانًا وَّبِذِى الْقُرْبٰى وَالْيَتٰمٰى وَالْمَسٰكِيْنِ وَالْجَارِ ذِى الْقُرْبٰى وَالْجَارِ الْجُنُبِ وَالصَّاحِبِ بِالْجَنْۢبِ وَابْنِ السَّبِيْلِ ۙ وَمَا مَلَكَتْ اَيْمَانُكُمْ ۗ اِنَّ اللّٰهَ لَا يُحِبُّ مَنْ كَانَ مُخْتَالًا فَخُوْرًا

"Worship Allah and associate nothing with Him, and to parents do good, and to relatives, orphans, the needy, the near neighbor, the neighbor farther away, the companion at your side, the traveler, and those whom your right hands possess. Indeed, Allah does not like those who are self-deluding and boastful." (Quran 4:36)

Allah (swt) has made it clear that we have responsibilities to other people, and that is where your community becomes important to you. If you are not aware of who is in your community and what their struggles are, how can you step up and help? It won't be enough to say we weren't aware of what was happening in our neighborhood, our community, or even in the world. We are tasked to be proactive to help people, whether they are Muslim or not.

Rights that our neighbors and community members have over us:[2]

1. Help them if they ask for help.

2. Provide relief if they seek it.

3. If they need a loan and you have the ability to help, lend them money.

4. Don't raise your building so high that you block their air without their consent.

5. Don't harass them.

6. Share your fruits with them. If you don't, make sure to bring it in your home without them seeing so they don't feel jealous.

---

2 Zakat, "Top 11 Rights Neighbors Have On You," https://www.zakat.org/top-11-rights-neighbors-understanding-muslims-duty-neighbors.

7. Visit them when they are ill.

8. Attend their funeral.

9. If they commit a sin, do not expose it if it is hidden.

10. Congratulate them if they get good news.

11. Be sympathetic if they face a calamity.

Exercise: Be a Good Neighbor

Have you ever met your neighbors? Do you know their names or what they do for a living? Have you ever sent them some food or a treat? Have you ever helped them out? If not, it's time to start. Write down the names of three of your neighbors and a little about them. Send all three of them a treat, just because!

NEIGHBOR	FUN FACTS	TREAT
1.		
2.		
3.		

The Good, the Bad, the Ugly

There are pros and cons to every situation, and being part of a community is no different. While there are so many benefits of having community support, it also means that there will be some pressures and trials that come with it as well. But we always aim to fulfill our responsibilities and turn to Allah (swt) for the bumps that come on the way.

New Muslims tend to face a lot of judgment and pressure from the community. When you deal with people, you also deal with their opinions, their expectations, their actions, and their words, which can get very difficult. You may hear contradictory opinions about the religion or face pressure to be an ideal Muslim. It's hard enough changing your lifestyle to fit into your new belief system, but having to hear judgment from others just creates an added layer of confusion.

New Muslims are not the only people who have to deal with the pressures of "what people think." This is a concept we grow up with, but the most important thing to remember is the only judgment and opinion that matters most is your Lord's, which is why it is so important to learn your religion and gain knowledge.

Knowledge isn't just power. It's confidence. It's strength. It's steadfastness.

Some of the pressures you may face as a new Muslim are:

* A revert will share their story.
* A revert will change their name to a "Muslim" name.
* A revert will get married as soon as possible if he or she is single.
* A revert will immediately take on the "appearance" of a Muslim.

Spill the Tea

As a new Muslim or even as someone who is getting back into the deen, you are always being asked your story.

What brought you to Islam? Who motivated you? Did something happen in your life that made you want to be a Muslim? What did you believe in before? Is your family supportive?

These are all very personal questions and sometimes as a community we think we have a right to this information. I don't think there are bad intentions here. People tend to be genuinely curious and inspired by reverts. New Muslims are truly a source of inspiration and a reminder to do better and be better. But even if the intention is good, the truth is you don't have to share your story if you don't want to.

Sometimes people just want too much information; they want the tea on everything that's going on in the community—who married who, who got into a fight, who got accepted into a school, who took off their hijab, and the list goes on. But being nosy is not encouraged in our religion at all. As a matter of fact, we are told to mind our own business and cover the faults of people. Allah (swt), our most Merciful Lord, wants us to conceal people's problems because that is having good character. But for some reason, people feel entitled to that information.

So if you feel pressure to share your story or your life, remember that your Lord has not asked you to, and He respects your privacy. Only share as much as you are comfortable with and learn to drown out the noise.

What's in a Name?

My name is my identity. It is an integral part of me, and it is the name my parents chose for me, not a task that parents take lightly. So why is it that people just assume you will change your name to a "Muslim" or Arabic-sounding name?

The truth is you don't have to.

I know many new Muslims do like to change their name, which is allowed, but you shouldn't feel pressured to do it. Your name is truly a part of your identity, and with all that is changing in your life, even though God willing it is for the better, it's okay to hold on to parts of your identity that make you feel comfortable. Changing your name is only recommended if the name you have is offensive in some way or has a bad meaning. Otherwise, the decision is yours.

Exercise: My Friends Call Me ...

Would you change your name if you could?   Yes ❑ No ❑

If yes, what would you change it to and why?

_____

_____

_____

What does your name mean?

_____

_____

_____

Why did your parents choose that name?

_____

_____

_____

Say I Do

A new Muslim, or any single Muslim over the age of 20, is almost always pressured to get married. Marriage is a beautiful thing, and it is highly recommended in Islam, though it is not required. You should never be pressured into it, especially if you are not ready.

For some reason, when there is a new eligible bachelor or bachelorette in the community, it's all we can talk about. I've known so many reverts who get married within the first six months of becoming a Muslim. There isn't anything wrong with this at all, but in my experience, I think it's important to take your time because new Muslims, especially women, are in a very vulnerable position.

The fact is that you are already in a transition period where a lot is changing and shifting in your life. It can be an amazing but also difficult time, especially after the initial "high" passes and everyday mundane life sets in. Instead of being treated as a person, reverts have said they end up feeling like shiny new toys. Everyone is really happy and wants to welcome them, but then they are left alone to figure things out for themselves once the initial excitement wears off.

To add on marriage, a huge blessing but a big responsibility into the mix while you are vulnerable, can make things more difficult, and it puts you in a position to be taken advantage of because you are still learning the deen. I've known many new Muslim women who were told by their new husbands what is right and wrong, what is allowed and not allowed, and how to practice when they get married too quickly after reverting. If you do want to get married sooner rather than later, then that is absolutely wonderful (I love a wedding as much as the next girl), but make sure it's actually what you want and not in answer to the pressure you are feeling.

In the Quran, Allah (swt) says:

وَمِنْ ءَايَـٰتِهِۦٓ أَنْ خَلَقَ لَكُم مِّنْ أَنفُسِكُمْ أَزْوَٰجًا لِّتَسْكُنُوٓا۟ إِلَيْهَا وَجَعَلَ بَيْنَكُم مَّوَدَّةً وَرَحْمَةً ۚ إِنَّ فِى ذَٰلِكَ لَءَايَـٰتٍ لِّقَوْمٍ يَتَفَكَّرُونَ ٢١

"And of His signs is that He created for you from yourselves mates that you may find tranquility in them; and He placed between you affection and mercy. Indeed in that are signs for a people who give thought." (30:21)

Your spouse is made for you to feel peace, affection, and mercy. So take your time discovering who can offer you the peace you need in your life, choosing the right person for yourself and getting to know their character in a halal manner.

Look the Part

Whether you are a Muslim woman or man, you are given certain guidelines in terms of dressing. In general, Muslim women are required to cover everything but their hands and face, and Muslim men are supposed to cover from navel to their knee. They are highly encouraged to keep a beard following the tradition of the Prophet (pbuh). We should always aim to follow the commands of Allah (swt) and try our best to please only Him.

What happens in our community is sometimes people want to see you apply all the commands of Allah (swt) all at once, or maybe you feel that pressure yourself. While it's amazing to do the best you can, it's important not to do so much at once that you end up giving up altogether. Anytime you start something new, whether you start working out or eating healthy or tackling a new job, you have to pace yourself so you stay consistent. So if you can't change your outer appearance all at once, that's okay.

Remember, you are a human being.

When it comes to how we look outwardly, judgment is so much easier because it's something everyone can see and have an opinion on. Aunties in the community might call you out for not wearing a hijab right away, or guys you hang out with will tell you to grow a beard. While the intentions may be good, the pressure and judgment can sometimes be too much.

The most important thing to do is gain knowledge and practice at your own pace. As you get closer to Allah (swt) and build your connection, your iman will increase and you'll naturally want to take steps to obey Allah's (swt) commands. What's more is that even born Muslims struggle with everyday commands, so it's important not to feel pressured to look and be perfect, because none of us are.

Exercise: Dressed to Impress

Are there changes you want to make to your outer appearance and dressing to be more pleasing to God? Yes ❏ No ❏

What changes do you want to make?

_____

_____

_____

_____

Make a plan and give yourself a deadline to make those changes.

_____

_____

_____

_____

_____

_____

_____

_____

Some of the expectations you will face are only human expectations and not expectations from Allah (swt), while others are indeed Allah's (swt) commands. Instead of falling into the pressure of people, it is better to take one step at a time and give yourself grace. To make your journey easier, become truly knowledgeable about what is actually an Islamic rule and what is a community pressure.

Chapter Summary Exercise: Never Stop Learning

What is something new I learned from this chapter, either about Islam or myself?

_____

_____

_____

_____

_____

_____

What am I grateful for today?

_____

_____

_____

_____

_____

_____

How did I lean on Allah (swt) today?

_____

_____

_____

_____

_____

Is there anyone I can forgive today? Or is there someone I should reach out to for forgiveness?

_____

_____

_____

_____

_____

Chapter 9

DUA: IT'S YOUR STRONGEST WEAPON

Dua is prayer.

As Muslims, we talk a lot about prayer, and it can mean many different things. Prayer can mean the five daily salah. Prayer is used for optional and extra salah. Prayer is used for worshiping Allah (swt). Prayer can mean talking to Allah (swt).

So what kind of prayer is dua?

Dua is when you pray to Allah (swt) to ask for whatever your heart desires. It is asking Allah (swt) to meet your needs. It is also a form of worship. Just raising our hands and asking for what we want is a good deed for us because it shows that we trust Allah (swt) and turn to Him when we have a request. It is how we show that we understand Allah (swt) is our Lord because no one else has the ability to give us what we need and answer our prayers. Dua is so special because it is making a request to the one who is capable of everything and the one who wants to answer our prayers, the one who has promised to respond to us.

In the Quran, Allah (swt) tells us:

وَقَالَ رَبُّكُمُ ٱدْعُونِى أَسْتَجِبْ لَكُمْ إِنَّ

"Your Lord has proclaimed, 'Call upon Me, I will respond to you.'" (Quran 40:60)

We are blessed to be able to ask Allah (swt) for everything we want, no matter how big or small it seems to us. It keeps us connected with our Lord. Dua is so strong and powerful that it is said to be able to change our qadr, our destiny. It can protect us from what is bad for us, and it can give us what is good for us.

But when do we tend to remember Allah (swt)? When do we turn to Him? When do we fall to our knees and beg Allah (swt) to help us and guide us and make things better?

When things are going wrong. When we are in a hardship. When we are being tested.

The truth is that when things are going well in our lives, we get so caught up in our happiness that we tend to forget about Allah (swt). We turn to him less, with weaker conviction, so when Allah (swt) loves us and remembers us, he lets some things go wrong so that we can turn to Him and build our connection with Him. And one of the best ways to do that is through dua.

Remember, nothing happens without Allah's (swt) will and decree. So if you have been allowed to make dua, if you have been guided to make dua, then it is certainly because Allah (swt) wants to accept your prayers and fulfill your needs.

وَإِذَا سَأَلَكَ عِبَادِى عَنِّى فَإِنِّى قَرِيبٌ ۖ أُجِيبُ دَعْوَةَ الدَّاعِ إِذَا دَعَانِ ۖ فَلْيَسْتَجِيبُوا لِى وَلْيُؤْمِنُوا بِى لَعَلَّهُمْ يَرْشُدُونَ ١٨٦

"When My servants ask you O Prophet about Me: I am truly near. I respond to one's prayer when they call upon Me. So let them respond with obedience to Me and believe in Me, perhaps they will be guided to the Right Way." (Quran 2:186)

In the Quran, Allah (swt) reminds us again and again that he *wants* to answer our prayers. Your Merciful Lord is waiting for you to simply ask so He can provide. What a mercy that truly is!

The wonderful thing about dua is that it is so accessible. You can make dua anytime, any place, in any language, in any way that you want. You can ask Allah (swt) while you are sitting, standing, or even lying down. Your Creator is always ready to listen, as long as you seek Him.

While dua can indeed be made however you want, there is some etiquette of dua that is encouraged, and if you can incorporate it as you make dua, your duas will be that much more effective.

Etiquettes of dua:

1. Start your dua by sending salawat, peace and blessings, on the Prophet (pbuh).

2. Use Allah's (swt) beautiful names to call Him.

3. Praise Allah (swt).

4. Face the qiblah, the direction of the Kaaba.

5. Raise your hands.

6. Have faith that your dua will be accepted; do not lose hope.

7. Ask frequently.

8. Ask with determination.

Exercise: Make Dua

Make dua. Write your duas to Allah (swt) and believe in your heart that they will come true. Call Allah (swt) by His beautiful names, seek forgiveness, and pour out your heart to your Lord.

_____

_____

_____

_____

_____

_____

_____

_____

The Rabanna Duas

Our duas can be said however we want. We can speak to God as a friend, we can cry to Him, we can seek Him in whichever way we like, but sometimes we are so lost and confused that we are at a loss of words. Sometimes we truly don't know what to ask. Sometimes we feel so bad about our sins or shortcomings that maybe we feel too embarrassed to ask. But our Merciful God has not left us on our own, even when it comes to asking for our wants and needs. Allah (swt) has shared beautiful duas in the Quran for us, and the Prophet (pbuh) taught as many duas as well, according to the hadith.

We aren't the only ones who feel this way from time to time. Even the prophets and messengers felt lost and confused and embarrassed sometimes, so Allah (swt) told them exactly what to say to Him. We are blessed to be able to use those same duas for ourselves as well.

The 40 *rabanna* duas are prayers that are from the Quran, and they all start with the word rabanna, meaning "Our Lord!" Here are just a few:

TYPE OF DUA	DUA
Dua for goodness in this world and the next	رَبَّنَا آتِنَا فِي الدُّنْيَا حَسَنَةً وَفِي الْآخِرَةِ حَسَنَةً وَقِنَا عَذَابَ النَّارِ *Rabbana atina fid dunyaa hasanatanw wa fil aakhirati hasanatanw wa qinaa azaaban Naar* "Our Lord, give us in this world [that which is] good and in the Hereafter [that which is] good and protect us from the punishment of the Fire." (Quran 2:201)
Dua for protection, patience and to be victorious Recited by Prophet Dawud (David)	رَبَّنَا أَفْرِغْ عَلَيْنَا صَبْرًا وَثَبِّتْ أَقْدَامَنَا وَانصُرْنَا عَلَى الْقَوْمِ الْكَافِرِينَ *Rabbana afrigh 'alainaa sabranw wa sabbit aqdaamanaa wansurnaa 'alal qawmil kaafireen* "Our Lord, pour upon us patience and plant firmly our feet and give us victory over the disbelieving people." (Quran 2:250)

TYPE OF DUA	DUA
Dua for repentance	رَبَّنَا لَا تُؤَاخِذْنَا إِن نَّسِينَا أَوْ أَخْطَأْنَا *Rabbana laa tu'aakhiznaaa in naseenaaa aw akhtaanaa* "Our Lord, do not impose blame upon us if we have forgotten or erred." (Quran 2:286)
Dua for provision	رَبَّنَا أَنزِلْ عَلَيْنَا مَائِدَةً مِّنَ السَّمَاءِ تَكُونُ لَنَا عِيدًا لِّأَوَّلِنَا وَآخِرِنَا وَآيَةً مِّنكَ ۖ وَارْزُقْنَا وَأَنتَ خَيْرُ الرَّازِقِينَ *Rabbanaaa anzil 'alainaa maaa'idatam minas samaaa'i takoonu lanaa 'eedal li awwalinaa wa aakhirinaa wa Aayatam minka warzuqnaa wa Anta khairur raaziqeen* "O Allah, our Lord, send down to us a table [spread with food] from the heaven to be for us a festival for the first of us and the last of us and a sign from You. And provide for us, and You are the best of providers." (Quran 5:114)
Dua for protection from bad companionship	رَبَّنَا لَا تَجْعَلْنَا مَعَ الْقَوْمِ الظَّالِمِينَ *Rabbanaa laa taj'alnaa ma'al qawmiz zaalimeen* "Our Lord, do not place us with the wrongdoing people." (Quran 7:47)
Dua for patience and a good death Recited by Prophet Musa (as)	رَبَّنَا أَفْرِغْ عَلَيْنَا صَبْرًا وَتَوَفَّنَا مُسْلِمِينَ *Rabbanaaa afrigh 'alainaa sabranw wa tawaffanaa muslimeen* "Our Lord, pour upon us patience and let us die as Muslims [in submission to You]." (Quran 7:126)
Dua showing tawakkul, complete trust in Allah (swt)	رَبَّنَا إِنَّكَ تَعْلَمُ مَا نُخْفِي وَمَا نُعْلِنُ ۗ وَمَا يَخْفَىٰ عَلَى اللَّهِ مِن شَيْءٍ فِي الْأَرْضِ وَلَا فِي السَّمَاءِ *Rabbanaaa innaka ta'lamu maa nukhfee wa maa nu'lin; wa maa yakhfaa 'alal laahi min shai'in fil ardi wa laa fis samaaa* "Our Lord, indeed You know what we conceal and what we declare, and nothing is hidden from Allah on the earth or in the heaven." (Quran 14:38)

TYPE OF DUA	DUA
Dua for us and our future generations to be righteous Recited by Prophet Ibrahim (as)	اِنّبَرِ جَاعَلْنِي مُقِيمَ الصّلاةِ وَمِن ذُرّيَّتِي ۚ رَبّنَا وَتَقَبّلْ دُعَآءِ *Rabbij 'alnee muqeemas Salaati wa min zurriyyatee Rabbanaa wa taqabbal du'aaa* "My Lord, make me an establisher of prayer, and [many] from my descendants. Our Lord, and accept my supplication." (Quran 14:40)
Dua for forgiveness for self and parents	اِنّبَر اغْفِرْ لِي وَلِوَالِدَيّ وَلِلْمُؤْمِنِينَ يَوْمَ يَقُومُ الْحِسَابُ *Rabbanagh fir lee wa liwaalidaiya wa lilmu'mineena Yawma yaqoomul hisaab* "Our Lord, forgive me and my parents and the believers the Day the account is established." (Quran 14:41)

When you make dua, you may not get exactly what you are asking for and there are many reasons for that. Sometimes what you want isn't the best for you. Allah (swt) knows best and will provide what is good. Allah (swt) knows what we don't, and sometimes, even if things don't make sense, it's vital to trust Allah's (swt) plan. So what happens if our dua doesn't come true? Was it a waste of time?

Of course not.

The three possibilities of dua:

1. Your dua will be answered.

2. You will receive something better in its place.

3. It will be saved for the afterlife, where you will get more.

Every dua, every tear, every cry, every request will be used for your benefit. No dua is ever said in vain. Therefore the outcome of dua is always positive.

Dua can be made in any way, any form, and through whatever feels comfortable to you. Your dua can be a conversation with Allah (swt) some days and a venting session other days. It can be a cry some days and it can be poem other days. Make dua in whatever way feels authentic to you in the moment that you are in. Since I love writing,

I really enjoy writing my duas down and going back to them from time to time. While some duas are specific and it's nice to go back to them and see if they came true—or if I was given something better in its place—some duas are timeless, and you can go back and make them over and over again.

During Ramadan many years ago, I wrote my duas into a poem that I go back to time and again because these are duas that I can always make in any time or space.

Dua of a Sinner

By Bisma Parvez

Oh Allah, my Creator, my Lord,

You are certainly the Knower of all.

How long has it been since I have spoken with You?

Surely, I have let myself fall.

Oh Merciful, my praise seems completely unfit,

How can Your humble servant honor You?

The inadequacy of my words leaves me feeling meek.

Do they even hold any value?

All praises are for You and You alone.

I do not deserve what I have been given.

Yet here I am, asking for more,

Regardless of my sins, I hope You will listen.

Ya Rabb,* Your slave turns obediently toward You,

In hopes of love and forgiveness.

My sins, so vast, take over my life,

And of that You are a witness.

Forgive my trespasses and replace them with good deeds

Though that is more than I deserve,

The tears in my eyes show my extreme regret

I pray in Jannah there is a place for me reserved.

My Lord, bestow upon me the wisdom and iman,

To truly live this dunya like a test.

I cannot fathom the tortures of the grave and hell

Protect me from such suffering, I request.

Forgive my eyes for what they have seen,

And my ears for what they have heard.

Forgive my tongue for the gossip and lies.

I wish I had not blundered.

My past, so tainted, haunts my thoughts,

I pray for a better life, this one and the next.

Love me and forgive me, regardless of my flaws,

And with me, do not be vexed.

Protect my family, my friends, and the Ummah,

Forgive our sins, the big and small,

The ones we insisted on, knowing they were wrong,

And even the ones we do not recall.

Grant us good deaths, as Muslims and Mu'minun,**

And take our souls with ease.

Let the last words we say be, "La illaha ill Allah."***

And let us enter Jannah without trial, please!

Wrap our bodies in a lovely scented cloth,

And let our angels be beautiful and bright.

Show us our places and homes in Jannah,

Ya Rabb, fill our spacious graves with light.

I know that I am certainly undeserving of this,

But You are surely Ar Rahman Ar Raheem,

So shower me with mercy, the limitless mercy You have,

And accept my duas. Ameen!

*Master or Lord

**True, successful believers

***Beginning of the shahada meaning "There is no God but Allah"

Chapter Summary Exercise: Never Stop Learning

What is something new I learned from this chapter, either about Islam or myself?

_____

_____

_____

_____

_____

_____

What am I grateful for today?

_____

_____

_____

_____

_____

_____

How did I lean on Allah (swt) today?

_____

_____

_____

_____

_____

Is there anyone I can forgive today? Or is there someone I should reach out to for forgiveness?

_____

_____

_____

_____

_____

Chapter 10

THIS IS ONLY THE BEGINNING

Life is a journey, not a destination.

The beauty of practicing our deen in this life is that it will never be complete on this Earth. No matter how much you learn, there will be more to understand. No matter how much you practice your faith, you can always be better. No matter how much you worship, you can always worship more.

Following your fitrah and finding your connection with your Lord is not the end. It's the first step of your real purpose: being a slave to nothing and no one except Allah (swt), our Merciful Lord who has promised to reward us with immense pleasures and beautiful gardens as long we can pass this little test called life.

Becoming a new Muslim is like having a clean slate. It's like being a newborn baby with no sins and a life ahead of you to gain the pleasure of Allah (swt). It is a true mercy and gift from your Creator because your past sins no longer count and you have the opportunity to be your best self. But that also means that there will be tests along the way.

As you continue down this new path, you will face different problems in your life—it's only natural. Because Allah (swt) loves us and wants us to remember Him, He will test us with trials and tribulations—some big and some small—but the goal is to always turn to Allah (swt) for help and reclaim our closeness. The goal is to have tawakkul.

Zoom Out

In some ways, we are all new Muslims because with each test, we renew our faith and connection to Allah (swt). There's a trick that I learned that has really helped me put my problems into perspective and continue to trust Allah (swt) as I renew my iman. Sometimes, our problems seem so big, so complicated and completely unsolvable. Sometimes our problem is all we can see and it seems like there is no solution at all. We start to feel hopeless. That's when I realize that I am focusing on the wrong thing.

The whole time, I've been so zoomed in with everything that has been going wrong that I forget about the thing that is right. I've been focusing on the problem when I should be focusing on the solution: Allah (swt).

Allah (swt) has the solution to our problems and Allah (swt) is the solution to our problems.

And so I imagine myself with a piece of paper in my hand held up right in front of my face, my eyes zooming in on words which state my problem. All I have to do is zoom out and drop the paper from in front of me, and realize that my solution is right behind it, and it is so massive it covers the horizon. And now that paper seems so small and insignificant because all I had to do was zoom out to realize I was focusing on the wrong thing. Allah (swt), who is infinitely bigger than everything, is right there waiting for me to lean on Him and ask Him to provide the solution.

So next time you are feeling like things aren't going right or your problem is too big to overcome, zoom out!

Falling Out of Orbit

Think back to when we talked about being a solar system. Becoming a new Muslim is deciding that something else is going to be the center of your system. You start orbiting something new—your Lord. Well, renewing your faith is similar, in a sense. Because as life goes on, our orbits can drift without us realizing it. The shift is so small and subtle that it isn't noticeable until a lot later. And theoretically we know we worship

Allah (swt), but our actions and thoughts might not reflect that as much as they should. So when we renew our faith, when we seek·closeness with Allah (swt) again, we're shifting our orbits once more to circle Allah (swt) correctly.

That's why this worldly journey is just the beginning, because we will drift and re-shift for the rest of our lives. So there's no rush. There's no race to the end. There's no pressure to be better than anyone. When there is no end, everything is the beginning. Your only competition is yourself to try and be better than the day you were before.

May Allah (swt) make us all successful on that journey.

Ameen!

Chapter Summary Exercise: Never Stop Learning

What am I grateful for today?

_____

_____

_____

_____

_____

What are practical steps I can take moving forward on my path to get closer to Allah (swt)?

_____

_____

_____

_____

_____

Where do you see yourself in the future when it comes to not just your dunya but also your deen?

Date: _____

QUESTION	RESOLUTIONS AND MANIFESTATION
Where do I see myself one month from today? What are my goals?	
Where do I see myself one year from today? What are my goals?	
Where do I see myself five years from today? What are my goals?	
Where do I see myself ten years from today? What are my goals?	

BIBLIOGRAPHY

"Five Pillars of Islam." Islamic Relief. Last updated March 8, 2023. https://www.islamic-relief.org.uk/resources/knowledge-base/five-pillars-of-islam.

"99 Names of Allah - Al Asma Ul Husna." Islamic Relief Canada, https://www.islamicreliefcanada.org/resources/99-names-of-allah.

Abdulla, Ahmed. "40 Rabbana Dua (Best Quranic Dua)." My Islam. October 17, 2019. https://myislam.org/40-rabbana-dua-best-quranic-dua.

Al-Ghazali, Abu Hamid. *The Book of Knowledge: Book 1 of the Revival of the Religious Sciences*. Louisville, KY: Fons Vitae Publishing, 2015.

Bensen, Patrick. "Tafsir of Surah Al-Kahf: The Story of Musa and Al-Khidr." Imam Ghazali Institute. March 5, 2021. https://www.imamghazali.org/blog/tafsir-surah-al-kahf-verses-60-82-musa-khidr.

"Breathing." Lung.ca. Accessed August 24, 2023. https://www.lung.ca/lung-health/lung-info/breathing.

Horoz, Tijen. "How to Perform Wudu." Muslim Hands. May 23, 2018. https://muslimhands.org.uk/latest/2018/05/how-to-perform-wudu.

"How to Perform Salah." Islamic Association of Raleigh. July 9, 2021. https://raleighmasjid.org/how-to-perform-salah.

Mogahed, Yasmin. *Reclaim Your Heart: Personal Insights on Breaking Free from Life's Shackles*. New York: IDIFY Publishing, 2015.

"Muslim Beliefs." BBC. https://www.bbc.co.uk/bitesize/guides/z43pfcw/revision/3. Accessed August 24, 2023.

"The Noble Quran." Quran.com. Accessed August 24, 2023. Quran.com.

Noormuhammad, Siddiq Osman. "Twenty Five Prophets Mentioned in the Holy Quran." Iqra Islamic Publications. http://www.iqra.net/articles/muslims/prophets.html. Accessed August 24, 2023.

"Top 11 Rights Neighbors Have on You." Zakat Foundation of America. Accessed August 24, 2023. https://www.zakat.org/top-11-rights-neighbors-understanding-muslims-duty-neighbors.

ACKNOWLEDGMENTS

I am deeply grateful to the following individuals, whose unwavering support and love have been instrumental in bringing this book to fruition:

Allah, My Merciful Lord: All praises are first and foremost to my Most Merciful Lord, without whom I am nothing and no one. I am grateful for every blessing and mercy in my life as I am a simple unworthy servant. I offer my deepest gratitude to Allah, the Almighty, whose grace and guidance have illuminated my path. I am profoundly thankful for the blessings and opportunities that have enabled me to share this work with the world.

Enaya Ansari: Thank you, my beloved daughter, Enaya, for being my source of hope and inspiration through your avid love for reading. I dedicate this work to you. Your caring and love fuel my every endeavor.

Ibrahim Ansari: To my dear son, Ibrahim, thank you for being my steadfast support and my motivator. Your encouragement has been a guiding light on this creative journey.

Saeeda Parvez: My heartfelt gratitude to my mother, Saeeda Parvez, for instilling in me the beauty and strength of Islam. Your dedication to our faith has shaped my spiritual path. I owe my profound love for Islam to your unwavering commitment.

Syed Parvez: To my father, Syed Parvez, whose sacrifice and strength laid the foundation for my life: You are my rock, and without you, I would not be where I am today. I learned about true love and felt it from you. Thank you for teaching me what it feels like to be loved unconditionally.

Tuba Parvez: My dear sister Tuba, thank you for always lifting me up during challenging times and being my most ardent supporter. Your belief in me has been a driving force.

Hiba Parvez: Thank you, my sister Hiba, for being a nurturing second mother and an exceptional role model. Your love and guidance have been invaluable throughout my journey.

Imad Parvez and Awais Parvez: To my dear brothers, Imad and Awais, I am grateful for your practical advice, unwavering motivation, and boundless love. Your presence in my life has been a constant source of strength.

Tania Yusaf and Esma Sherwani: To my sweet sisters-in-law, Tania and Esma, I am thankful for your kind words of encouragement and for always having your doors open to me and my children.

Sofia Zaidi, Saher Khan, Neda Khan, Fatima Malik, Hera Arham, and Zaynab Salman: Heartfelt appreciation to my cherished friends and mentors, Sofia, Saher, Neda, Fatima, Hera, and Zaynab. Allah placed you all in my life for very specific reasons at the perfect time. Your presence in my life has been a pillar of strength. Thank you for the laughter, guidance, and unwavering encouragement. You've played a vital role in reminding me of my worth, giving me confidence when I felt low, keeping me on the right path, and reminding me to trust in my Lord at one point or another in my life.

Renee Rutledge and Claire Sielaff: To my incredible editors, Renee Rutledge and Claire Sielaff, I extend my sincere gratitude. Your patience and guidance have shaped this book into what it is today. I am honored to have worked with such amazing women.

Yasmin Mogahed: A special acknowledgment to Yasmin Mogahed, whose profound words and books have provided solace during my darkest hours. Your wisdom has been a guiding light on my spiritual journey.

Fahad Ansari: Last but most certainly not least, I want to thank you, Fahad. You showed me the world in more ways than one. You opened my eyes to Allah's beautiful creations and taught me about things I would never come across on my own. Most importantly, because of you, I learned how to use my heart. You came into my life to teach me to love myself and to rely solely on my Lord. I believe Allah chose you for me because you were able to teach me about my own strength, resilience, and kindness. Because of you, my heart was opened to Allah's mercy and love. I wouldn't know what tawakkul is without you, and for that I am forever grateful.

ABOUT THE AUTHOR

As a Pakistani Muslim American, Bisma Parvez is a passionate content creator, influencer, and writer dedicated to sharing her diverse lifestyle, heritage, and profound faith through the lens of social media. A proud mother of two, Bisma finds immense joy and purpose in nurturing her family while championing the beauty and values of her Muslim faith. Previously a reporter at the *Detroit Free Press* and *Bridge Detroit*, Bisma covered breaking news, politics, and underrepresented communities. Now, as a writer and influencer, Bisma seeks to redefine the narrative surrounding Muslims and Islam.